THE LIVING CHURCH BOOKS

Christianity today is confronted by such challenges that all Christians need to be well informed about the truths, strengths and enjoyments which are theirs in their heritage. They need to know, too, about the many experiments and reassessments which are renewing the Church for its mission in the contemporary world. Our aim in the Living Church Books is to contribute to the intensive educational effort which the crisis demands.

THE
REFORMED PASTOR

RICHARD BAXTER

Edited by
HUGH MARTIN
C.H., D.D.

SCM PRESS LTD
BLOOMSBURY STREET LONDON

First published in this edition 1956
Second impression 1963
Printed in Great Britain by
Billing and Sons Ltd., Guildford and London

CONTENTS

[5]

CHAPTER TWO
THE OVERSIGHT OF THE FLOCK

CHAPTER THREE

APPLICATION

EDITOR'S FOREWORD

R I C H A R D B A X T E R represents Puritanism at its best, and more of the essential man is perhaps to be found in *The Reformed Pastor* than in any other of his numerous books, with the possible exception of his *Autobiography*. Born in 1615 and dying in 1691, he was alive in one of the stormiest and most creative periods in English history. He was a chaplain in the Parliamentary army in the Civil War, very distrustful of Charles I though with little love for Cromwell, lived through the Commonwealth and took a leading part in the recall of Charles II. Though he was himself episcopally ordained and had, in fact, recently declined an invitation to become bishop of Hereford, he could not in conscience accept the requirement, laid down in 1662—for the first time in England since the Reformation—that episcopal ordination was essential for the Christian ministry. Nor could he declare that the Book of Common Prayer was perfect beyond criticism and that he would never seek its revision. So, with some 1,800 others, he sorrowfully became a nonconformist, and suffered much persecution, distraint and imprisonment.

He was a learned man with a broad outlook and an eager interest in all that was going on around him, in politics, in the new sciences, and in literature. But above all he was a zealous pastor and preacher, all the more zealous because he believed that his very precarious health presaged an early death. His ministry in the parish church at Kidderminster was one of the most noteworthy in Christian history. The bitterest fruit of his nonconformity was that he was forbidden to preach. Believing in a 'moderate episcopacy' and an ordered liturgy, he tried to take the middle road between the 'sects' and the episcopalian conformists, and so intercepted the fire from both sides. His eagerness often overmastered his tact, and even when he tried to promote reconciliation his olive branches were apt to be fired from a catapult.[1] He played a great part in the political, theological and religious life of England, and the influence of his writings was powerful for generations after his death.[2]

The Reformed Pastor, written in 1655 when Baxter was forty-one, is one of his most famous and influential books. He called it originally by the odd title of *Gildas Salvianus or The Reformed Pastor*, after two early writers who also used great plainness of speech in castigating the sins of their generations. 'By their names I offer you an excuse for plain dealing.' But even on the title page of the first edition the words *Reformed Pastor* stand out in the biggest type and by common consent it has always been so called. By 'reformed' Baxter did not mean 'Protestant', but 'recalled to faithful service'. 'If God would but reform the ministry,' he wrote in his *Autobiography*, 'and set them on their duties zealously and faithfully, the People would certainly be reformed. All Churches either rise or fall as the ministry doth rise or fall (not in riches or worldly grandeur) but in knowledge, zeal and ability for their work.' Nothing could describe more pithily the theme of his *Reformed Pastor*. That the ministry

[1] Newman's witty comment on Pusey's *Eirenicon*.
[2] For a fuller account of the man and his work reference may be permitted to the present editor's book, *Puritanism and Richard Baxter* (S.C.M. Press).

in general sadly needed reformation in the seventeenth century is borne out by much contemporary evidence, a fact which needs to be kept in mind in reading Baxter's strictures. It should be remembered also that the book as Baxter wrote it is in large part devoted to the discussion of 'church discipline' and individual pastoral work. This has been mostly omitted in this edition as not relevant to-day. But it should be realized that Baxter is not only an upholder of lofty ideals and a searching critic : he is offering helpful practical advice from an experienced minister in the conduct of congregational life. This book has searched the hearts of generations of Christian ministers and rekindled the flame of service. It is worthy of attention by the layman also. One of the attractive features of the edition edited by J. T. Wilkinson for the Epworth Press is the Introductory Essay in which he brings together many illustrations of its influence through three hundred years.

Editors have had to take liberties with Baxter's writings, but he suffers less than most from being cut. He was a wordy, repetitive and long-winded author. This was partly because he was in a hurry to get his message on paper, and partly because of his conviction that you have to say a thing at least three times before most people take it in. While there are in his writings many passages of splendid prose, Baxter scorned to polish and ornament what he wrote, and in his haste, to tell the truth, was often clumsy. From these faults *The Reformed Pastor* is by no means free. Yet, for all that, Baxter 'speaks things', as Carlyle said of Cromwell, and few can match him for forcefulness.

But though some editing of Baxter is inevitable for any modern republication I had not realized to what an extent editors have in fact interfered with *The Reformed Pastor* by drastic rearrangement and 'bowdlerizing' until, in preparing this edition, I was able by the courtesy of Dr Williams' Library to compare several later versions with the original. Some regrouping of the material is very desirable to overcome its repetitiveness, and in this I have been glad to follow in large measure the work of the Rev. William Brown, M.D. (Fifth edition, 1862). But Brown's constant paraphrasing of Baxter's words is often quite gratuitous and dulls the colour and force of the original. I have made my own selection of passages and have allowed Baxter to write his own book in his own words, even at some cost in neatness and polish and the preservation of some now archaic expressions. I have, however, modernized the spelling. Some words from Dr Brown's preface I make my own: 'Though considerably less than the original (this edition) has been reduced in size chiefly by the omission of extraneous and controversial matter, which however useful when the work was originally published, is for the most part inapplicable to the circumstances of the present age.' The original is a volume of about 550 closely printed pages.

Baxter gives his own account of the occasion of the book in his Preface.[1] Behind his criticism and advice lies the experience and authority of his remarkable ministry at Kidderminster. He reproaches some of his brother ministers with being dull and drowsy preachers. At least there is no drowsiness here. The book blazes with white-hot zeal, evangelistic passion, and eagerness to convince his readers. And he has still much to say to us.

HUGH MARTIN.

[1] See p. 13 below, and also the Appendix, p. 123.

THE PREFACE

TO MY REVEREND AND DEARLY BELOVED BRETHREN, THE
FAITHFUL MINISTERS OF CHRIST IN BRITAIN AND IRELAND,
GRACE AND PEACE IN JESUS CHRIST BE INCREASED.

REVEREND BRETHREN,

The subject of this Treatise so nearly concerneth yourselves and the churches committed to your care, that it
persuadeth and emboldeneth me to this address, notwithstanding the imperfections in the manner of handling it,
and the consciousness of my great unworthiness to be your
monitor.

Before I come to my principal errand, I shall give you an
account of the reasons of this following work, and of the
freedom of speech, which to some may be displeasing.

When the Lord had awakened His ministers in this
County and some neighbouring parts to a sense of their
duty in the work of catechizing and private instruction of
all in their parishes that would not obstinately refuse their
help, and when they had subscribed an Agreement[1] containing their resolutions for the future performance of it,
they judged it unmeet to enter upon the work without a
solemn humbling of their souls before the Lord, for their
long neglect of so great and necessary a duty; and
therefore they agreed to meet together at Worcester,
December 4th, 1655, and there to join in such humiliation, and in earnest prayer to God for the pardon of

[1] See p. 123 below.

[13]

our neglects, and for His special assistance in the
work that we had undertaken, and for the success of
it with the people whom we are engaged to instruct;
at which time, among others, I was desired by them to
preach. In answer to their desires I prepared the following
discourse; which though it proved longer than could be
delivered in one or two sermons, yet I intended to have
entered upon it at that time, and to have delivered that
which was most pertinent to the occasion, and reserved
the rest to another season. But before the meeting, by the
increase of my ordinary pain and weakness, I was disabled
from going thither. To recompense which unwilling
omission, I easily yielded to the requests of divers of the
brethren, forthwith to publish the things which I had prepared, that they might *see* that which they could not *hear*.

If now it be objected, that I should not have spoken so
plainly or sharply against the sins of the ministry, or that I
should not have published it to the view of the world, or
at least that I should have done it in another tongue and
not in the ears of the vulgar, I confess I thought the
objection very considerable; but that it prevailed not to
alter my resolution is to be ascribed to the following
reasons. 1. It was a purposed solemn Humiliation that we
were agreed on, and that this was prepared and intended
for. And how should we be humbled without a plain confession of our sin? 2. It was principally our own sins that
the confession did concern; and who can be offended with
us for confessing our own, and taking the blame and shame
to ourselves which our consciences told us we ought to do.
3. I have excepted in our confessions those that are
not guilty: and therefore hope that I have injured none.
4. Having necessarily prepared it in the English tongue I
had no spare time to translate it. 5. Where the sin is open

in the sight of the world it is in vain to attempt to hide it. 6. And such attempts will but aggravate it and increase our shame. 7. A free confession is a condition of a full remission and when the sin is public the confession must be public. If the ministers of England had sinned only in Latin, I would have made shift here to admonish them in Latin,[1] or else have said nothing to them. But if they will sin in English, they must hear of it in English. Unpardoned sin will never let us rest and prosper, though we be at never so much care and cost to cover it; our sin will surely find us out. If we be so tender of ourselves and so loath to confess, God will be the less tender of us. I think it is no time now to stand upon our credit, so far as to neglect our duty and befriend our sins. It rather beseems us to fall down at the feet of our offended Lord and to justify Him in His judgments, and freely and penitently to confess our transgressions, and to resolve upon a speedy and thorough reformation. Certainly as repentance is necessary to the recovery of our peace with God, so it is also to the reparation of our credit with wise and godly men. Our penitent confession and speedy reformation are the means that must silence the reproaching adversaries.

The leaders of the flock must be exemplary to the rest; and therefore in this duty as well as in any other. It is not our part only to teach them repentance, but to go before them in the exercise of it ourselves As far as we excel them in knowledge and other gifts, so far should we also excel them in this and other graces. How can we more effectually further a reformation (which we are so much obliged to

[1] Not such a fanciful suggestion as it would be to-day. Latin was still the international language of theology and Baxter himself wrote at least one considerable book in it. As it is, *The Reformed Pastor* itself contains numerous long Latin quotations.

do) than by endeavouring the reforming of the leaders of the Church? For my part I have done as I would be done by; and it is for God and the safety of the Church, and in tender love to the brethren, whom I do adventure to reprehend that so no enemy may find this matter of reproach amongst us. But especially because our faithful endeavours are of so great necessity to the welfare of the Church, and the saving of men's souls, that it will not consist with a love to either, to be negligent ourselves, or silently to connive and comply with the negligent.

If thousands of you were in a leaking ship, and those that should pump out the water and stop the leaks should be sporting or asleep, yea, or but favour themselves in their labours, to the hazarding of you all, would you not awake them to their work, and call out on them to labour as for your lives? And if you used some sharpness and importunity with the slothful, would you think that man were well in his wits that would take it ill of you, and accuse you of pride, self-conceitedness, or unmannerliness to talk so saucily to your fellow workmen? or should tell you that you wrong them by diminishing their reputation? Would you not say: 'The work must be done, or we are all dead men: is the ship ready to sink and do you talk of reputation?: or had you rather hazard yourself and us, than hear of your slothfulness?' This is our case, brethren. The work of God must needs be done: souls must not perish while you mind your worldly business, and take your ease, or quarrel with your brethren: nor must we be silent while men are hastened by you to perdition, and the Church to greater danger and confusion.

If your own body be sick, and you will despise the remedy; or if your own house be on fire, and you will be singing or quarrelling in the streets, I can possibly bear it,

[16]

and let you alone—which yet in charity I should not easily do. But if you will undertake to be the physician of an hospital, or to all the town that is infected with the plague; or will undertake to quench all the fires that shall be kindled in the town, there is no bearing with your remissness, how much soever it may displease you. I speak all this to none but the guilty; and thus I have given you those reasons which forced me, even in plain English, to publish so much of the sins of the ministry, as in the following treatise I have done.

I never intended in urging the peace and unity of the saints to approve of anything which I judged to be a sin, nor to tie my own tongue or other men's from seasonable contradicting it. Is there no way to peace but participating of men's sins? The thing I desire is this: 1. That we might all consider how far we might hold communion together, even in the same congregations, notwithstanding our different opinions; and to agree not to withdraw where it may possibly be avoided. 2. But where it cannot, that we may consult how far we may hold communion in separate congregations; and to avoid that no further than is of mere necessity. And 3, and principally, to consult and agree upon certain rules for the management of our differences in such a manner as may be least to the disadvantage of the common Christian truths which are acknowledged by us all. Thus far would I seek peace with Arminians, Antinomians, Anabaptists, or any that holds the foundation. Yea, and in the two last I would not refuse to consult on accommodation with moderate Papists themselves, if their principles were not against such consultations and accommodations.

I crave your candid interpretation of my boldness, assuring you that I bear not the counsel of my flesh herein,

B

but displease myself as much as some of you: and had rather have the ease and peace of silence, if it would stand with duty and the Church's good. But it is the mere necessity of the souls of men, and my desire of their salvation and the prosperity of the Church, which force me to this arrogancy and immodesty, if so it must be called. For who that hath a tongue can be silent, when it is for the honour of God, the welfare of His Church and the everlasting happiness of so many persons?

And the first and main matter which I have to propound to you is, whether it not be the unquestionable duty of the generality of ministers to set themselves presently[1] to the work of catechizing and personal instructing all that are to be taught by them, who will be persuaded to submit thereunto? Can you think that holy wisdom will gainsay it? If there be a thousand or five hundred ignorant[2] people in your parish, it is a poor discharge of your duty now and then occasionally to speak to some few of them and let the rest alone in their ignorance, if you can afford them help. Will it satisfy you to deal with one person of twenty or forty or a hundred and to pass by all the rest? I do now, in the behalf of Christ, and for the sake of His Church and the immortal souls of men, beseech all the faithful ministers of Christ that they will presently and effectually fall upon this work. Combine for a unanimous performance of it, and it may more easily procure the submission of your people. I am far from presuming to prescribe you rules or forms, or so much as to motion to you to tread in our steps, in any circumstances where a difference is tolerable, or to use the same catechism or exhortation as we do: only fall presently and closely to

[1] i.e. immediately.
[2] i.e. religious truth.

the work. This duty hath its rise from the Lord and is generally approved by His Church. And for my part, let them and spare not, tread me in the dirt, and let me be as vile in their eyes as they please, so they will but listen to God and reason and fall upon the work, that our hopes of a more common salvation of men and of a true reformation of the Church may be revived.

I must confess that I find by some experience, that this is the work that must reform indeed and must make true godliness a commoner thing. Indeed I do admire[1] at myself how I was kept off from so clear and excellent a duty so long. I was long convinced of it, but my apprehensions of the difficulties were too great, and my apprehensions of the duty too small: that so I was hindered long from the performance. I thought that the people would but have scorned it, and none but a few that had least need would have submitted to it. I was long detained in delays, which I beseech the Lord of mercy to forgive. Whereas upon trial, I find the difficulties almost nothing, save only through my extraordinary bodily weakness, to that which I imagined; and I find the benefits and comforts of the work to be such that I profess, I would not wish that I had forborne it for all the riches in the world (as for myself). We spend Monday and Tuesday from morning to almost night in the work, taking about fifteen or sixteen families in a week, that we may go through the parish, which hath above eight hundred families, in a year; and I cannot say yet that one family hath refused to come to me, nor but few persons excused and shifted it off. And I find more outward signs of success with most that come, than of all my public preaching to them. If you ask me what course I take for order and expedition, in a word, at the delivery of the catechisms, I

[1] i.e. wonder.

take a catalogue of the persons of understanding in the parish and the clerk goeth a week before to every family to tell them when to come and at what hour (one family at eight o'clock, the next at nine, and the next at ten, etc.). And I am forced by the number to deal with a whole family at once, but admit not any of another to be present.

Brethren, do I now invite you to this work without God or without the consent of your own consciences? You have put your hand to the plough of God; you are doubly sanctified and devoted to Him as Christians and pastors; and dare you, after this, draw back and refuse His work? You see the work of reformation at a stand; and you are engaged by many obligations to promote it; and dare you now neglect those means by which it must be done? I dare prognosticate, from the knowledge of the nature of grace, that all the godly ministers in England will make conscience of this duty and address themselves to it. I do not hopelessly persuade you to it; but take it for granted it will be done.

My second request to the reverend ministers in these nations is that they would, without any more delay, unanimously set themselves to the practice of those parts of Christian discipline, which are unquestionably necessary. I now beseech you that would make a comfortable account to the chief Shepherd and would not be found unfaithful in the house of God.

My third and last request is, that all the faithful ministers of Christ, would, without any more delay, unite and associate for the furtherance of each other in the work of the Lord and the maintenance of unity and concord in His Churches; and that they would not neglect their brotherly meetings to those ends, nor yet spend them unprofitably, but improve them to their edification and effectual carrying on the work. And let none draw back that accord in the substantials of faith and godliness. Yea if some should think themselves necessitated (I will not say to schism, lest I offend them, but) to separate in public worship from the rest, methinks, if they be indeed Christians, they should be willing to hold so much communion with them as they can, and to consult how to manage their differences to the least disadvantage to the common truths and Christian cause which they all profess to own and prefer.

Brethren, I crave your pardon for the infirmities of this address, and earnestly longing for the success of your labours I shall daily beg of God, that He would persuade you to those duties which I have here requested you to perform, and would preserve and prosper you therein, against all the serpentine subtlety and rage that is now engaged to oppose and hinder you.

Your unworthy fellow-servant,

RICH. BAXTER

April 15, 1656.

TO THE LAY READER

I INTEND, if God enable me and give me time, a second part, containing the duty of the people in relation to their pastors, and therein to show the right and necessity of a ministry; the way to know which is the true church and ministry and how we justify our own calling to this office, and how false prophets and teachers must be discerned; how far the people must assist the pastors in the Gospel and the pastors put them on and make use of them to that end; how far the people must submit to their pastors, and what other duty they must perform in that relation. But because my time and strength are so uncertain that I know not whether I may live to publish my yet imperfect preparations on this subject, I dare not let this first part come into your hands without a word of caution and advice, lest you misunderstand or misapply it.

Entertain not any unworthy thoughts of your pastors, because we here confess our own sins. You know it is men and not angels that are put by God in the office of church guides; and you know that we are imperfect men. We believe that he that saith he hath no sin, deceiveth himself, and the truth is not in him (I John 1.8). And we profess to know but in part, and to have our treasure in earthen vessels, and to be insufficient for these things. And therefore see that you love and imitate the holiness of your pastors, but take not occasion of disesteeming or reproaching them for their infirmities. Let me tell you that for all the sins of the ministry which we have here confessed, the known world hath not a more able, faithful, godly ministry than Britain hath at this day.

See that you obey your faithful teachers and improve their help for your salvation. Take heed that you refuse not to learn when they would teach you. And in particular, see that you refuse not to submit to them in this duty of private instruction which is mentioned in this treatise. Go to them when they desire you and be thankful for their help. Yes, and at other times when you need their advice, go to them of your own accord and ask it; their office is to be your guides in the way of life. I shall say no more to you on this point, but only desire you to read and consider the exhortation which is published in our *Agreement*[1] itself; and if you read this book, remember that the duty which you find to belong to the ministers doth show also what belongs to yourselves.

RICH. BAXTER

April, 1656.

[1] See pp. 123-126 below.

TAKE HEED THEREFORE UNTO YOURSELVES, AND TO ALL THE FLOCK, OVER WHICH THE HOLY GHOST HATH MADE YOU OVERSEERS, TO FEED THE CHURCH OF GOD, WHICH HE HATH PURCHASED WITH HIS OWN BLOOD.

ACTS 20.28.

CHAPTER ONE

THE OVERSIGHT OF OURSELVES

Reverend and dearly-beloved Brethren,

Though some think that Paul's exhortation to these elders doth prove him their ruler, we who are this day to speak to you from the Lord, hope that we may freely do the like, without any jealousies of such a conclusion. Though we teach our people, as officers set over them in the Lord, yet may we teach one another, as brethren in office, as well as in faith. If the people of our charge must 'teach and admonish and exhort each other daily', no doubt teachers may do it to one another, without any super-eminency of power or degree. We have the same sins to kill and the same graces to be quickened and corroborated, as our people have: we have greater works than they to do, and greater difficulties to overcome, and therefore we have need to be warned and awakened, if not to be instructed, as well as they. So that I confess I think such meetings should be more frequent, if we had nothing else to do together but this. And as plainly and closely should we deal with one another, as the most serious among us do with our flocks; lest if only they have the sharp admonitions and reproofs, they only should be sound and lively in the faith. That this was Paul's judgment, I need no other proof, than this rousing, heart-melting exhortation to the Ephesian elders. A short sermon, but not soon learnt. Had the bishops and teachers of the Church but thoroughly learned this short exhortation, though with the neglect of many a volume which hath taken up their time, and helped them to greater applause in the world, how happy had it been for the Church and themselves!

My text, supposing Paul the speaker and the Ephesian elders his hearers, containeth, 1. A twofold duty. 2. A fourfold motive to enforce it. The first duty is, to take heed to ourselves. The second is, to take heed to all the flock. And the main work for the flock which is thus heedfully to be done, is expressed, even to feed them, or play the shepherds for them.

The motives closely laid together are these. 1. From their engagement and relation: they are the overseers of the flock; it is their office. 2. From the efficient cause; even the authority and excellency of Him that called them to it, which was the Holy Ghost. 3. From the dignity of the object, which is the matter of their charge; it is the Church of God, the most excellent and honourable society in the world. 4. From the tender regard that Christ hath to this Church, and the price it cost Him; He purchased it with His own blood.

Episkopous, bishops or overseers here, were officers appointed to teach and guide those Churches in the way to salvation, and it is the same persons that are called elders of the Church of Ephesus before, and bishops here. Of whom more anon. The verb seemeth here to import both the qualification, ordination, and particular designation of these elders or bishops to their charge, for we must not limit and exclude without necessity. The Holy Ghost did by all these three ways make them overseers of their flocks. 1. By qualifying them with such gifts as made them fit for it. 2. By directing the minds of those that ordained them to the ministry. 3. By disposing both their own minds, and the ordainers, and the peoples for the affixing them to that particular church rather than another.

It is necessary before we proceed to instruction and application, that we be resolved more clearly who those elders or bishops be that Paul doth here exhort. I am desirous to do all that lawfully I may to avoid controversy, especially in this place, and on such occasions. But here it is unavoidable, because all our following application will much depend upon the explication: and if you shall once suppose that none of this exhortation was spoken to men in your office and capacity, no wonder if you pass it over and let it alone and take all that I shall hence gather for your practice, as impertinent. This text was wont to be thought most apt to awaken the ministers of the Gospel to their duty; but of late the negligent are gratified with the news (for news it is) that only bishops in a supereminent sense, whom we usually call prelates, are spoken to in this text; and not only so, but that no other text of scripture doth speak to any other church-presbyters (certainly) but them; yea, that no other were in being in Scripture times.

[Baxter urges, against Irenaeus, that these elders were all from the single Church at Ephesus.]

We are agreed now that they were the same persons who in Scripture are called 'bishops' and 'presbyters'. And that these persons had the power of ordination and jurisdiction. And that these persons were not the bishops of many particular churches, but one only. That is, they ruled the particular churches just as our parish pastors do. So that we are satisfied that we go the way that the apostles established. Yet not presuming to censure all superior episcopacy, nor refusing to obey any man that commandeth us to do our duty, but resolving to do our own work in faithfulness and peace.

For my own part, I have ever thought it easier to be governed than to govern; and I am ready to be obedient to any man in and for the Lord. Were Christ's work but thoroughly done, I should be the backwardest in contending who should have the doing of it. Let but able, faithful men be the overseers, that will make the Word of God the rule, and lay out themselves for the saving of men's souls, and I am resolved never to contend with such about the business of superiority; but cheerfully to obey them in all things lawful, if they require my obedience. Would they but lay by all needless human impositions and obstructions, and be contented with the sufficient word of God, and not make new work to necessitate new canons and authorities to impose it, but be content with the Gospel simplicity, and let us take that for a sufficient way to heaven, that Peter and Paul went thither in, I think I should not disobey such a bishop, though I were not satisfied of his differing order or degree. But enough of this.

Section *1*.   *The Nature of this oversight*

Let us consider, What it is to take heed to ourselves.

A. See that the work of saving grace be thoroughly wrought in your own souls. Take heed to yourselves lest you be void of that saving grace of God which you offer to others and be strangers to the effectual working of that Gospel which you preach; and lest while you proclaim the necessity of a saviour to the world your own heart should neglect Him and His saving benefits. Take heed to yourselves lest you perish while you call upon others to take heed of perishing; and lest you famish yourselves while you prepare their food. Though there be a promise of shining as the stars to those that turn many to righteousness, that is but on the supposition that they are first turned to it themselves. Their own sincerity in the faith is the condition of their glory, simply considered, though their great ministerial labours may be a condition of the promise of their greater glory. Many a man hath warned others that they come not to that place of torment, which yet they hasted to themselves: many a preacher is now in hell, that hath a hundred times called upon his hearers to use the utmost care and diligence to escape it. Can any reasonable man imagine that God should save men for offering salvation to others, while they refused it themselves; and for telling others those truths which they themselves neglected and abused? Many a tailor goes in rags, that maketh costly clothes for others; and many a cook scarce licks his fingers, when he hath dressed for others the most costly dishes. Believe it, brethren, God never saved any man for being a preacher, nor because he was an able preacher; but because he was a justified, sanctified man, and consequently faithful in His Master's work. Take heed, therefore, to yourselves first, that you be that which you persuade your hearers to be, and believe that which you persuade them to believe, and have heartily entertained that Christ and spirit which you offer unto others. He that bid you love your neighbours as yourselves, did imply that you should love yourselves, and not hate and destroy yourselves and them.

It is a fearful case to be an unsanctified professor,[1] but much more to be an unsanctified preacher. Doth it not make you tremble when you open the Bible, lest you should read there the sentence of your own condemnation?

[1] i.e. one who makes profession of being a Christian.

When you pen your sermons, little do you think that you are drawing up indictments against your own souls! When you are arguing against sin, that you are aggravating your own! When you proclaim to your hearers the riches of Christ and grace, you publish your own iniquity in reject-ing them, and your unhappiness in being without them! What can you do in persuading men to Christ, in drawing them from the world, in urging them to a life of faith and holiness, but conscience, if it were awake, would tell you that you speak all this to your own confusion. A graceless, inexperienced[1] preacher is one of the most unhappy creatures upon earth: and yet he is ordinarily most insensible of his unhappiness; for he hath so many counters that seem like the gold of saving grace, and so many splendid stones that seem like the Christian's jewel that he is seldom troubled with the thoughts of his poverty; but thinks he is 'rich and increased in goods and stands in need of nothing' when he is 'poor and miserable and blind and naked'. He is acquainted with the Holy Scriptures, he is exercised in holy duties, he liveth not in open disgraceful sin, he serveth at God's altar, he reproveth other men's faults, and preacheth up holiness both of heart and life; and how can this man choose but be holy? Oh what aggra-vated misery is this, to perish in the midst of plenty and to famish with the bread of life in our hands, while we offer it to others, and urge it on them! That those ordi-nances of God should be the occasion of our delusion, which are instituted to be the means of our conviction and salvation! and that while we hold the looking-glass of the Gospel to others, to show them the face and aspect of their souls, we should either look on the back part of it ourselves, where we can see nothing, or turn it aside,

[1] i.e. without personal experience of God in his own life.

that it may misrepresent us to ourselves! If such a wretched man would take my counsel, he should make a stand, and call his heart and life to an account, and fall a preaching awhile to himself, before he preach any more to others.

[Baxter here introduces an appeal to 'all our students in the university' to realize that the personal knowledge of God is the foundation of all true learning.] What a poor business is it to themselves to spend their time in knowing some little of the works of God, and some of those names that the divided tongues of the nations have imposed on them, and not to know the Lord Himself nor exalt Him in their hearts. Nothing can be rightly known if God be not known! nor is any study well managed, nor to any great purpose, where God is not studied. We know little of the creature till we know it as it standeth in its order and respects to God: single letters and syllables uncomposed are nonsense. He that overlooketh the Alpha and Omega and seeth not the beginning and end and Him who is the all of all, doth see nothing at all. All creatures are as such broken syllables; they signify nothing as separated from God. Were they separated actually they would cease to be and the separation would be an annihilation. And when we separate them in our fancies, we make nothing of them to ourselves. It is one thing to know the creatures as Aristotle, and another thing to know them as a Christian. None but a Christian can read one line of his physics so as to understand it rightly. It is an high and excellent study and of greater use than many do well understand; but it is the smallest part of it that Aristotle can teach us.

When man was made perfect and placed in a perfect world, where all things were in perfect order and very good, the whole of creation was then man's book in which he was to read the nature and will of his great Creator. And if man had held on in this prescribed work he would have continued and increased in the knowledge of God and himself; but when he would needs know and love the creature and himself in a way of separation from God, he lost the knowledge both of the creature and of the Creator, so far as it was worth the name of knowledge.

I hope you perceive what all this driveth at, namely that to see God in His creatures and to love Him and converse with Him, was the employment of man in his upright state; that this is so far from ceasing to be our duty that it is the work of Christ by faith to bring us back to it; and there-fore the most holy men are the most excellent students of God's works. 'His works are great, sought out by all them that have pleasure therein'; but not for themselves, but for Him that made them. Your study of physics and other sciences is not worth a rush, if it be not God by them that you seek after. To see and admire, to reverence and adore, to love and delight in God appearing to us in His works, and purposely to peruse them for the knowledge of God, this is the true and only philosophy. This is the sanctifi-cation of your studies, when they are devoted to God, and when He is the life of them all, and they all intend Him as the end and the principal object.

And, therefore, I presume to tell you by the way, that it is a grand error, and of dangerous consequence in Christian academies (pardon the censure from one so unfit for it, seeing the necessity of the case commandeth it) that they study the creature before the Redeemer, and set themselves to physics and metaphysics before they set themselves to theology; when as no man that hath not the vitals of theology is capable of going beyond a fool in philosophy.[1]

B. Content not yourselves to have the main work of grace, but be also very careful that your graces be kept in life and action, and that you preach to yourselves the sermons that you study, before you preach them to others. If you did this for your own sakes, it would not be lost labour; but I am speaking to you upon the public account, that you would do it for the sake of the Church. When your minds are in a heavenly, holy frame, your people are like to partake of the fruits of it. Your prayers and praises and doctrine will be heavenly and sweet to them. They will likely feel when you have been much with God: that which is on your hearts most is like to be most in their ears. I confess I must speak of it by lamentable experience, that I publish to my flock the distempers of my soul. When I let my heart grow cold, my preaching is cold; and when it is confused, my preaching will be so; and so I can observe too oft in the best of my hearers, that when I have a while grown cold in preaching, they have cooled accordingly, and the next prayers which I have heard from them have been too like my preaching. We are the nurses of Christ's little ones. If we forbear our food they will quickly find it in the want of milk. We shall famish them and we may quickly see it again on them in their lean and dull discharge of their several duties. If we let our love go down

---

[1] It is interesting to remember in this connection that Baxter was noted for his keen interest in the lively developments of the natural sciences in his day. Boyle, the famous chemist, was a devoted Christian and a close friend of Baxter. He sent a cordial reply to a letter from Baxter expressing great interest in his experiments: 'There are divers things that bespeak you to be none of these narrow-souled divines that by too much suspecting Natural Philosophy, tempt many of its votaries to suspect Theology.'

C

we are not like to raise up theirs. If we feed on unwhole-some food, either errors or fruitless controversies, our hearers are like to fare the worse for it. Whereas if we could abound in faith and love and zeal, how would it over-flow to the refreshing of our congregations. O brethren, watch therefore over your own hearts : keep out lusts and passions and worldly inclinations; keep up the life of faith and love; be much at home and be much with God. If it be not your daily business to study your own hearts and subdue corruptions and live as upon God, if you make it not your very work to which you constantly attend, all will go amiss, and you will starve your auditors; or if you have but an affected fervency, you cannot expect such a blessing to attend it. Be much, above all, in secret prayer and meditation. There you must fetch the heavenly fire that must kindle your sacrifices : remember you cannot decline and neglect your duty to your own hurt alone but many will be losers by it as well as you. For your people's sake, therefore, look to your hearts.

And, more particularly, methinks a minister should take some special pains with his heart, before he is to go to the congregation : if it be then cold, how is he likely to warm the hearts of the hearers? Therefore go then specially to God for life and read some rousing, awakening book, or meditate on the weight of the subject that you are to speak of, and on the great necessity of your people's souls, that you may go in the zeal of the Lord into His house.

C. Take heed to yourselves lest your example contradict your doctrine, and lest you lay such stumbling blocks before the blind as may be the occasion of their ruin : lest you unsay with your lives what you say with your tongues; and be the greatest hinderers of the success of your own labours. It much hindereth our work when other men are all the week long contradicting to poor people in private that which we have been speaking to them from the Word of God in public, because we cannot be at hand to expose their folly; but it will much more hinder if we contradict ourselves, and if our actions give our tongue the lie, and if you built up an hour or two with your mouths, and all the week after pull down with your hands! This is the way to make men think that the word of God is but an idle tale, and to make preaching seem no better than prating. He that means as he speaks, will sure do as he speaks.

It is a palpable error in those ministers that make such a disproportion between their preaching and their living; that they will study hard to preach exactly, and study little or not at all to live exactly. They are loath to misplace a word in their sermons, or to be guilty of any notable infirmity (and I blame them not, for the matter is holy and weighty), but then make nothing of misplacing affections, words and actions in the course of their lives. O how curiously[1] have I heard some men preach; and how carelessly have I seen them live! Certainly, brethren, we have very great cause to take heed what we do, as well as what we say: if we will be the servants of Christ indeed, we must not be tongue servants only, but must serve Him with our deeds, and be 'doers of the work that we may be blessed in our deed'. As our people must be 'doers of the word and not hearers only'; so we must be doers and not speakers only, lest we 'deceive our own selves'. A practical doctrine must be practically preached. We must study as hard how to live well, as how to preach well. O brethren! it is easier to chide at sin than to overcome it.

Do well as well as say well: be zealous of good works.

[1] i.e. with what great care.

Spare not for any cost, if it may promote your Master's work.

Maintain your innocency, and walk without offence. Let your lives condemn sin, and persuade men to duty. Would you have your people be more careful of their souls, than you will be of yours? If you would have them redeem their time, do not you mis-spend yours. If you would not have them vain in their conference, see that you speak yourselves the things which may edify, and tend to minister grace to the hearers. Order your own families well if you would have them do so by theirs. Be not proud and lordly if you would have them to be lowly. There is no virtue wherein your example will do more, at least to abate men's prejudice, than humility, and meekness, and self-denial. Forgive injuries, and be not overcome of evil, but overcome evil with good; do as our Lord, who when He was reviled, reviled not again. If sinners be stubborn, and stout, and contemptuous, flesh and blood will persuade you to take up their weapons, and master them by their carnal means: but that's not the way (further than necessary self-preservation or public good requireth it), but overcome them with kindness, and patience, and gentleness. The former may shew that you have more worldly power than they (wherein yet they are ordinarily too hard for the faithful); but it's the latter only that will tell them that you overtop them in spiritual excellency, and in the true qualifications of a saint. If you believe that Christ was more imitable than Caesar or Alexander, and that it is more glory to be a Christian than to be a conqueror, yea to be a man than a beast (who oft exceed us in strength), contend then with charity, and not with violence; and set meekness, and love, and patience against force, and not force against force. Remember you are obliged to be the servants of all. Condescend to men of low estate; be not strange to the poor ones of your flock. They are apt to take your strangeness for contempt : familiarity improved to holy ends, is exceeding necessary, and may do abundance of good. Speak not stoutly or disrespectfully to any one; but be courteous to the meanest as your equal in Christ. A kind and winning carriage is a cheap way of advantage to do men good.

D. Lastly, take heed to yourselves that you be not unfit for the great employments that you have undertaken. He must not himself be a babe in knowledge that will teach men all those mysterious things that are to be known in order to salvation. Oh what qualifications are necessary for a man who hath such a charge upon him as we have! How many difficulties in divinity to be opened; and these too about the very fundamentals that must needs be known. How many obscure texts of Scripture to be expounded. How many duties to be done, wherein ourselves and others may miscarry, if in the matter and end and manner they be not well informed. How many sins to be avoided which without understanding and foresight cannot be done. What a number of sly and subtle temptations must we open to our people's eyes, that they may escape them. How many weighty and yet intricate cases of conscience have we almost daily to resolve. Can so much work and such work as this be done by raw, unqualified men?

What skill doth every part of our work require—and of how much moment is every part. To preach a sermon, I think, is not the hardest part; and yet what skill is necessary to make plain the truth, to convince the hearers, to let in unresistible light into their consciences and to keep it there and drive all home, to screw the truth into their minds and work Christ into their affections, to meet every objection and clearly to resolve it, to drive sinners to a stand and make them see that there is no hope, but that they must unavoidably be converted or condemned; and to do all this so for language and manner as beseems our work, and yet as is most suitable to the capacities of our hearers. This, and a great deal more that should be done in every sermon should sure be done with a great deal of holy skill. So great a God whose message we deliver, should be honoured by our delivery of it. It is a lamentable case that in a message from the God of heaven, of everlasting consequence to the souls of men, we should behave ourselves so weakly, so unhandsomely, so imprudently, or so slightly, that the whole business should miscarry in our hands and God be dishonoured, and His work disgraced, and sinners rather hardened than converted.

O brethren, do you not shrink and tremble under the sense of all this work? Will a common measure of holy skill and ability, of prudence and other qualifications, serve for such a task as this? I know necessity may cause the Church to tolerate the weak; but woe to us, if we tolerate and indulge our own weakness! Do not reason and conscience tell you that if you dare venture on so high a work as this, you should spare no pains to be fitted to perform it? It is not now and then an idle snatch or taste of studies that will serve to make a sound divine. I know that laziness hath learned to pretend the lowness of all our studies, and how wholly and only the Spirit must qualify and assist us to the work—as if God commanded us the use of means and then would warrant us to neglect them. As if it were His way to cause us to thrive in a course of idleness, and to bring us to knowledge by dreams when we are asleep, or to take us up into heaven, and show us His counsels, while we think of no such matter, but are idling away our time! Oh that men should dare so sinfully by their laziness to quench the Spirit and then pretend the Spirit for the doing of it! God hath required us that we be 'not slothful in business' but 'fervent in spirit, serving the Lord'. Such we must provoke our hearers to be; and such we must be ourselves. Oh, therefore, brethren, lose no time! Study and pray and confer and practise; for by these four ways your abilities must be increased. Take heed to yourselves, lest you are weak through you own negligence, and lest you mar the work of God by your weakness.

Section 2.   *The Motives to this Oversight*

Having showed you what it is to take heed to yourselves, I shall next lay before you some motives to awaken you to this duty.

A. You have a heaven to win or lose yourselves, and souls that must be happy or miserable for ever; and therefore it concerneth you to begin at home, and to take heed to yourselves as well as unto others. Preaching well may succeed to the salvation of others, without the holiness of your own hearts and lives; it is possible at least, though less usual; but it is impossible it should serve to save yourselves. 'Many will say in that day, Lord, Lord, have we not prophesied in thy name' who shall be answered with an 'I never knew you. Depart from me, ye that work iniquity.' O sirs, how many men have preached Christ and perished for want of a saving interest in Him! How many that are now in hell, have told their people of the torments of hell and warned them to avoid it! How many have preached of the wrath of God against sinners, who are now feeling it! Oh what sadder case can there be in the world, than for a man that made it his very trade and calling to proclaim salvation and to help others to attain it, yet after all to be himself shut out! Alas, that ever we should have so many books in our libraries which tell us the way to heaven; that we should spend so many years in reading these books and studying the doctrine of eternal life, and after all this to miss it! That ever we should study and preach so many sermons of damnation and yet fall into it! And all because we preached so many sermons of Christ while we neglected Him, of the Spirit, while we resisted Him, of faith, while we did not heartily believe, of repentance and conversion, while we continued in the state of flesh and sin, and of a heavenly life, while we remained carnal and earthly ourselves. If we will be divines only in tongue and title, and have not the divine image upon our souls, nor give up ourselves to the divine honour and will, no wonder if we be separated from the Divine presence and denied the fruition of God for ever. Believe it, sirs, God is no respecter of persons: He saveth not men for their coats or callings; a holy calling will not save an unholy man. If you stand at the door of the kingdom of grace, to light others in, and will not go in yourselves, you shall knock in vain at the gates of glory, that would not enter at the door of grace.

B. Take heed to yourselves, for you have a depraved nature, and sinful inclinations, as well as others. If innocent Adam had need of heed, and lost himself and us for want of it, how much more need have such as we! Sin dwelleth in us, when we have preached never so much against it; and one degree prepareth the heart for another, and one sin inclineth the mind to more. If one thief be in the house, he will let in the rest; because they have the same disposition and design. A spark is the beginning of a flame; and a small disease may cause a greater. A man who knows himself to be purblind, should take heed to his feet. Alas! even in our hearts as well as in our hearers, there is an averseness to God, a strangeness to Him, unreasonable and almost unruly passions! In us there is, at the best, the remnants of pride, unbelief, self-seeking, hypocrisy, and all the most hateful, deadly sins. And doth it not then concern us to take heed?

C. Take heed to yourselves, because the tempter will make his first and sharpest onset upon you. If you will be the leaders against him, he will spare you no further than God restraineth him. He beareth you the greatest malice that are engaged to do him the greatest mischief. As he hateth Christ more than any of us, because He is the General of the field and the Captain of our salvation, and doth more than all the world besides against the kingdom of darkness; so doth he hate the leaders under Him more than the common soldiers: he knows what a rout he may make among the rest if the leaders fall before their eyes. He hath long tried that way of fighting, neither against great or small comparatively, but of smiting the shepherds that he may scatter the flock: and so great hath been his success this way that he will follow it on as far as he is able. Take heed, therefore, brethren, for the enemy hath a special eye upon you. You shall have his most subtle insinuations and incessant solicitations and violent assaults. As wise and learned as you are, take heed to yourselves lest he overwit you. The devil is a greater scholar than you, and a nimbler disputant: he can transform himself into an angel of light to deceive: he will get within you and trip up your heels before you are aware: he will play the juggler with you undiscerned, and cheat you of your faith or innocency, and you shall not know that you have lost it; nay, he will make you believe it is multiplied or increased when it is lost. You shall see neither hook nor line, much less the subtle angler himself, while he is offering you his bait. And his bait shall be so fitted to your temper and disposition, that he will be sure to find advantages within you, and make your own principles and inclinations to betray you. Oh what a conquest will he think he hath got, if he can make a minister lazy and unfaithful, if he can tempt a minister into covetousness or scandal.

D. Take heed to yourselves, because there are many eyes upon you, and there will be many observers of your falls. You cannot miscarry but the world will ring of it. The eclipses of the sun by day time are seldom without witnesses. As you take yourselves for the lights of the churches, you may expect that men's eyes should be upon you. If other men may sin without observation, so cannot you. And you should thankfully consider how great a mercy this is, that you have so many eyes to watch over you, and so many to tell you of your faults; and thus have greater helps than others, at least for the restraining of your sin. Though they may do it with a malicious mind, yet you have the advantage of it. God forbid that we should prove so impudent as to do evil in the public view of all, and to sin wilfully while the world is gazing on us. Take heed therefore to yourselves and do your works as those that remember that the world looks on them, and that with the quicksighted eye of malice, ready to make the worst of all, and to find the smallest fault where it is, and aggravate it where they find it, and divulge it and make it advantageous to their designs, and to make faults where they cannot find them.

E. Take heed to yourselves, for your sins have more

heinous aggravations than other men's. It was a saying of King Alphonsus that 'a great man cannot commit a small sin'. We may much more say that a learned man, or a teacher of others, cannot commit a small sin; or at least that the sin is great as committed by him, which is smaller in another.

You are more likely than others to sin against knowledge, because you have more than they. At least, you sin against more light or means of knowledge. What, do you not know that covetousness and pride are sins? Do you not know what it is to be unfaithful to your trust and by negligence or self-seeking to betray men's souls? You know your Master's will; and if you do it not, you shall be beaten with many stripes. There must needs be the more wilfulness, by how much there is the more knowledge. If you sin, it is because you *will* sin.

Your sins have more hypocrisy in them than other men's, by how much the more you have spoken against them. Oh what a heinous thing is it in us, to study how to disgrace sin to the utmost and make it as odious in the eyes of our people as we can, and when we have done, to live in it and secretly cherish that which we openly disgrace! What vile hypocrisy is it to make it our daily work to cry it down and yet to keep to it, to call it publicly all naught, and privately to make it our bedfellow and companion, to bind heavy burdens on others and not to touch them ourselves with a finger.

F. Take heed to yourselves because such work as ours do put men on greater use and trial of their graces and have greater temptations than many other men's. Weaker gifts and graces may carry a man through in a more even course of life, that is not put to so great trials. Smaller strength may serve for lighter work and burdens. But if you will

venture on the great undertakings of the ministry, if you
will lead on the troops of Christ against the face of Satan
and his followers, if you will engage yourselves against
principalities and powers and spiritual wickedness in high
places, if you undertake to rescue captivated sinners and
to fetch men out of the devil's paws; do not think that a
heedless, careless minister is fit for so great a work as this.
You must look to come off with greater shame and deeper
wounds of conscience than if you had lived a common life,
if you will think to go through such things as these with
a careless soul. It is not only the work that calls for heed
but the workman also, that he may be fit for business of
such weight. We have seen by experience that many men
that lived as private Christians in good reputation for parts
and piety, when they have taken upon them either the
military employment or magistracy, where the work was
above their parts and temptations did overmatch their
strength, they have proved scandalous disgraced men. And
we have seen some private Christians of good note that,
having thought too highly of their parts, and thrust themselves into the ministerial office, they have been empty
men, and almost burdens to the Church. They might have
done God more service in the higher rank of private men,
than they do among the lowest of the ministry. If you will
venture into the midst of the enemies and bear the burden
and heat of the day, take heed to yourselves.

G. Take heed to yourselves; for the honour of your Lord
and Master and of His holy truth and ways, doth lie more
on you than other men. As you do Him more service, so
also more disservice than others. The nearer men stand to
God, the greater dishonour hath He by their miscarriages;
and the more will they be imputed by foolish men to God
Himself. The heavy judgment was threatened and executed

on Eli and on his house because they kicked at His sacrifices and offerings: 'Therefore was the sin of the young men very great before the Lord, for men abhorred the offering of the Lord' (I Sam. 2.12 ff.). It was the great aggravation of 'causing the enemies of the Lord to blaspheme' which provoked God to deal more sharply with David than else He would have done (II Sam. 12.14). If you are indeed Christians, the glory of God will be dearer to you than your lives. Take heed, therefore, what you do against it, as you would take heed what you do against your lives. Would it not wound you to the heart to hear the name and truth of God reproached for your sakes?

H. Lastly, take heed to yourselves, for the success of all your labours doth very much depend on this. God useth to fit men for great works, before He will make them His instruments in accomplishing them. If the work of the Lord be not soundly done upon your own hearts, how can you expect that He will bless your labours for effecting it in others? He may do it if He please, but you have much cause to doubt whether He will.

None but the upright do make God their chief end, and do all or anything heartily to His honour; others make the ministry but a trade to live by. They choose it rather than another calling, because their parents did destinate them to it and it is a life wherein they have more opportunity to furnish their intellects with all kind of science; and because it is not so toilsome to the body, to those that have a will to favour their flesh; and because it is accompanied with some reverence and respect from men, and because they think it a fine thing to be leaders and teachers and have others receive the law at their mouths; and because it affordeth them a competent maintenance. For such ends as these are they ministers and for these do they preach; and were it not for these and such as these they would soon give over. And can it be expected that God will bless the labours of such men as these? It is not for Him they preach but for themselves and their own reputation or gain. And though many of these men may seem excellent preachers, and may cry down sin as loud as others, yet it is all but an affected fervency, and too commonly but a mere ineffectual bawling. For he that cherisheth sin in his own heart doth never fall upon it in good earnest in others. A traitorous commander that shooteth against the enemy nothing but powder, may cause his guns to make as great a sound or report as some that are laden with bullets; but he doeth no hurt to the enemy. So one of these men may speak as loudly and mouth it with an affected fervency; but he seldom doth any great execution against sin and Satan.

It is not likely that people will regard much the doctrine of such men when they see that they do not live as they preach. They will think that he doth not *mean* as he speaks, if he *do* not as he speaks. They will hardly believe a man that seemeth not to believe himself. If a man bid you run for your lives because a bear or an enemy is at your backs, and yet do not mend his pace himself, you will be tempted to think that he is but in jest and that there is really no such danger as he pretends. When preachers tell people of the necessity of holiness, and that without it no man may see the Lord, and yet remain unholy themselves, the people will think that they do but talk to pass away the hour, and because they must say somewhat for their money, and that all these be but words of course. All that a preacher doth is a kind of preaching; and when you live a covetous or a careless life, you preach these sins to your people by your practice.

That man, therefore, that is not himself taken up with

the predominant love of God, and is not himself devoted to Him and doth not devote to Him all that he hath and can do; that man that is not addicted to the pleasing of God and maketh Him not the centre of all his actions, and liveth not to him as his God and happiness; that is, that man that is not a sincere Christian himself, is utterly unfit to be a pastor of a church. No man is fit to be a minister of Christ that is not of a public spirit as to the Church and delighteth not in its beauty and longeth not for its felicity. As the good of the Commonwealth must be the end of the magistrate (his nearer end) so must the felicity of the Church be the end of the pastor of it. So that he must rejoice in its welfare and be willing to spend and be spent for its sake.

No man is fit to be a pastor of a church that doth not set his heart on the life to come, and regard the matters of everlasting life above all the matters of this present life; and that is not sensible in some measure how much the inestimable riches of glory are to be preferred to the trifles of this world. For he will never set his heart on the work of men's salvation that doth not heartily believe and value that salvation.

He that delighteth not in holiness, hateth not iniquity, loveth not the unity and purity of the Church, and abhorreth not discord and divisions, and taketh not pleasure in the communion of saints and the public worship of God with his people, is not fit to be a pastor of a church. For none of all these can have the true ends of a pastor, and therefore cannot do the work.

CHAPTER TWO

THE OVERSIGHT OF THE FLOCK

Section 1. The Nature of this Oversight

HAVING showed you what it is to take heed to your-selves, I am to show you next what it is to take heed to all the flock.

The ultimate end of our pastoral oversight, is that which is the ultimate end of our whole lives; even the pleasing and glorifying of God, and the glorification of His Church. And the nearer ends of our office, are the sanctification and holy obedience of the people of our charge, their unity, order, beauty, strength, preservation and increase; and the right worshipping of God, especially in the solemn assemblies.

The subject matter of the ministerial work is, in general, spiritual things, or matters that concern the pleasing of God, and the salvation of our people. It is not about tem-poral and transitory things. Our business is not to dispose of commonwealths, nor to touch men's purses or persons by our penalties: but it consisteth only in these two things:

1. In revealing to men that happiness, or chief good, which must be their ultimate end.

2. In acquainting them with the right means for the attainment of this end, and helping them to use them, and hindering them from the contrary.

1. It is the first and great work of the ministers of Christ to acquaint men with that God made them, and is their happiness: to open to them the treasures of His goodness, and tell them of the glory that is in His presence, which all His chosen people shall enjoy: that so by shewing men the certainty and excellency of the promised felicity, and the perfect blessedness in the life to come, compared with the vanities of this present life, we may turn the stream of their cogitations and affections, and bring them to a due contempt of this world, and set them on seeking the durable treasure.

2. Having shewed them the right end, our next work is to acquaint them with the right means of attaining it. Where the wrong way must be disgraced, the evil of all sin must be manifested, and the danger that it hath brought us into, and the hurt it hath already done us, must be discovered. Then have we the great mystery of redemption to disclose; the person, natures, incarnation, perfection, life, miracles, sufferings, death, burial, resurrection, ascension, glorification, dominion, intercession of the blessed Son of God. As also the tenor of His promises, the conditions imposed on us, the duties which He hath commanded us, and the everlasting torments which He hath threatened to the final impenitent neglecters of His grace. O what a treasury of His blessings and graces and the privileges of His saints have we to unfold! What a blessed life of holiness and communion therein have we to recommend to the sons of men! And yet how many temptations, difficulties and dangers to disclose, and assist them against! How much of their own corruptions and sinful inclinations to discover and root out! We have the depths of God's bottomless love and mercy, the depth of the mysteries of His designs, and works of creation, redemption, providence,

D

justification, adoption, sanctification, glorification; the depth of Satan's temptations, and the depth of their own hearts, to disclose. In a word, we must teach them, as much as we can, of the whole word and works of God. O what two volumes are there for a minister to preach upon! How great, how excellent, how wonderful and mysterious! All Christians are disciples or scholars of Christ, the Church is His school; we are His ushers, the Bible is His grammar: this is what we must be daily teaching them.

All the flock, even each individual member of our charge, must be taken heed of and watched over by us in our ministry. To which end it is necessary that we should know every person that belongeth to our charge. For how can we take heed to them if we do not know them? We must labour to be acquainted with the state of all our people as fully as we can, with their inclinations and conversations; to know what are the sins they are most in danger of, and what duties they neglect and what temptations they are most liable to. For if we know not their temperament or disease we are like to prove but unsuccessful physicians.

All the flock being thus known, must afterward be heeded. One would think all reasonable men would be satisfied of this, and it should need no further proof. Doth not a careful shepherd look after every individual sheep? and a good schoolmaster look to every individual scholar? and a good physician look after every particular patient? and good commanders look after every individual soldier? Why then should not the teachers, the pastors, the physicians, the guides of the churches of Christ, take heed to every individual member of their charge? Christ Himself, the great and good Shepherd, that hath the whole to look after, doth yet take care of every individual. In the fifteenth of Luke He telleth us that He is as the shepherd that leaves

' the ninety and nine sheep in the wilderness, to seek after one that was lost '. The prophets are often sent to individual men. Ezekiel is made a watchman over individuals, and must say to the wicked, ' Thou shalt surely die.' Paul taught them ' publicly and from house to house ', which was meant of his teaching particular families. The same Paul ' warned every man and taught every man in all wisdom, that he might present every man perfect in Christ Jesus ', Many more passages of Scripture assure us that it is our duty to take heed to every individual person in our flock. And many passages in the ancient councils do plainly tell us it was the practice of those times; but I shall mention only one passage in Ignatius : ' Let assemblies ', says he, ' be often gathered; inquire after all by name : despise not servant-men or maids.' You see it was then taken for a duty to look after every member of the flock by name, though it were the meanest servant-man or maid.

But while it is our duty to take heed to all the flock, we must pay special attention to some classes in particular. By many this is very imperfectly understood, and therefore I shall dwell a little upon it.

A. We must labour, in a special manner, for the conversion of the unconverted.

The work of conversion is the first and great thing we must drive at; after this we must labour with all our might. Alas! the misery of the unconverted is so great, that it calleth loudest to us for compassion. If a truly converted sinner do fall, it will be but into sin which will sure be pardoned, and he is not in that hazard of damnation by it as others are. Not but that God hateth their sins as well as others, or that He will bring them to heaven let them live ever so wickedly; but the spirit that is within them will not suffer them to live wickedly nor to sin as the ungodly do. But with the unconverted it is far otherwise. They 'are in the gall of bitterness and the bond of iniquity', and have yet no part nor fellowship in the pardon of their sins or the hopes of glory. We have, therefore, a work of greater necessity to do for them, even 'to open their eyes and to turn them from darkness to light, and from the power of Satan unto God; that they may receive forgiveness of sins, and an inheritance among them that are sanctified', He that seeth one man sick of a mortal disease and another only pained with the toothache, will be moved more to compassionate the former than the latter; and will sure make more haste to help him, though he were a stranger and the other were a son. It is so sad a case to see men in a state of damnation, wherein, if they should die, they are remedilessly lost, that methinks we should not be able to let them alone, either in public or private, whatever other work we may have to do. I confess, I am forced frequently to neglect that which should tend to the further increase of knowledge in the godly, because of the lamentable necessity of the unconverted.

B. We must be ready to give advice to those that come to us with cases of conscience, especially the great case which the Jews put to Peter, and the gaoler to Paul and Silas, 'What must we do to be saved?' A minister is not only for public preaching, but to be a known counsellor for their souls, as the lawyer for their estates, and the physician for their bodies: so that each man that is in doubt and straits may bring his case to him and desire resolution; as Nicodemus came to Christ, and as it was usual for the people to go to the priest, 'whose lips must keep knowledge and at whose mouth they must ask the law, because he is the messenger of the Lord of hosts'. And because the people are grown unacquainted with this office of the ministry, and their own necessity and duty herein, it belongeth to us to acquaint them herewith and to press them publicly to come to us for advice in such uses of great concernment to their souls. We must not only be willing of the trouble, but draw it upon ourselves by inviting them hereto. What abundance of good we might do, could we but bring our people to this. And, doubtless, much might be done in it, if we did our duties. How few have I ever heard of who have heartily pressed their people to duty in this. A sad case that men's souls should be so injured and hazarded by the total neglect of so great a duty, and that ministers scarce ever tell them of it and awaken them to it. Were they but duly sensible of the need and weight of this, you should have them more frequently knocking at your doors and making their sad complaints and begging your advice. I beseech you put them more on this for the future; and perform it very carefully when they seek your help. To this end it is very necessary that we be acquainted with the nature of true grace, and able to assist them in trying their states and in resolving the main question that concerns their everlasting life or death. One word of seasonable, prudent advice given by a minister to persons in necessity hath done that good that many sermons would not have done. 'A word fitly spoken,' says Solomon, 'how good is it.'

C. The next part of the ministerial work is for the building of those that are already truly converted. And according to the various states of these, the work is various.

1. There are many of our flock that are weak, who, though they are of long standing, are yet of small proficiency or strength. And indeed, it is the most common condition of the godly. Most of them stick in weak and

low degrees of grace, and it is no easy matter to get them higher. To bring them to higher and stricter opinions is easy, that is, to bring them from the truth into error, on the right hand as well as on the left; but to increase their knowledge and gifts is not easy, and to increase their graces is the hardest of all. It is a very troublesome thing to be weak: it keepeth under dangers, it abateth consolations and delight in God, and taketh off the sweetness of His ways—it maketh us less serviceable to God and man, to bring less honour to our Master, and to do less good to all about us. We get small benefit in the use of the means of grace. We too easily play with the serpent's baits, and are ensnared by his wiles. A seducer will easily make us shake, and evil may be made to appear to us as good, truth as falsehood, sin as duty; and so on the contrary. We are less able to resist and stand in an encounter; we sooner fall; we hardlier rise; and are apter to prove a scandal and reproach to our profession. We less know ourselves, and are more apt to be mistaken as to our own estate, not observing corruptions when they have got advantage. We are dishonourable to the Gospel by our very weakness, and little useful to any about us, and in a word, though we live to less profit to ourselves or others, yet are we unwilling and too unready to die.

And, seeing the case of weakness is so sad, how diligent should we be to cherish and increase their grace! The strength of Christians is the honour of the Church. When men are inflamed with the love of God, and live by a lively working faith, and set light by the profits and honours of the world, and love one another with a pure heart fervently, and can bear and heartily forgive a wrong, and suffer joyfully for the cause of Christ, and study to do good, and walk inoffensively and harmlessly in the world, as ready to be servants to all men for their good, becoming all things to all men in order to win them, and yet abstaining from the appearance of evil, and seasoning all their actions with a sweet mixture of prudence, humility, zeal, and heavenly spirituality, oh, what an honour are such to their profession! What ornaments to the Church, and how excellently serviceable to God and man! Men would sooner believe that the Gospel is indeed a word of truth and power if they could see such effects of it upon the hearts and lives of men. The world is better able to read the nature of religion in a man's life than in the Bible. They that obey not the word, may be won by the conversation[1] of such as these. It is, therefore, a necessary part of our work, to labour more in the polishing and perfecting of the saints, that they may be strong in the Lord, and fitted for their Master's use.

2. Another sort of converts that need our special help, are those that labour under some particular distemper that keeps under their graces, and maketh them temptations and troubles to others, and a burden to themselves. For, alas, too many such there are; some that are specially addicted to pride and some to worldliness and some to this or that sensual desire, and many to frowardness and disturbing passions. It is our duty to set in for the assistance of all these; and partly by dissuasions and clear discoveries of the odiousness of the sin, and partly by suitable directions about the way of remedy, to help them to a more complete conquest of their corruptions. We are leaders of Christ's army against the power of darkness and must resist all the works of darkness wherever we find them, though it be in the children of light. We must be no more

---

[1] In the seventeenth century, and in the Authorized Version, ' conversation ' meant ' manner of life ', not only talking.

tender of the sins of the godly than of the ungodly, nor any more befriend them or favour them. By how much more we love their persons by so much the more must we express it in the opposition of their sins. And yet we must look to meet with some tender persons here, especially when iniquity hath got any head, and made a party, and many have fallen in love with it. They will be as pettish and impatient of reproof as some worser men, and interest piety itself into their faults. But the ministers of Christ must do their duties for all men's peevishness; and must not so far hate their brother as to forbear the plain rebuking of him, or suffer sin to lie upon his soul. Though it must be done with much prudence, yet done it must be.

3. Another sort that our work is about is declining Christians, that are either fallen into some scandalous sin, or else abate their zeal and diligence, and show us that they have lost their former love. As the case of backsliders is very sad, so our diligence must be very great for their recovery. It is sad to them to lose so much of their life and peace and serviceableness to God; and to become so serviceable to Satan and his cause. It is sad to us to see that all our labour is come to this; and that when we have taken so much pains with them and had such hopes of them, all should be so far frustrated. It is saddest of all to think God should be so abused by those that He hath so loved and done so much for, and that Christ should be so wounded in the house of a friend, and the name of God evil spoken of among the wicked. Besides such partial backsliding hath a natural tendency to total apostasy and would effect it, if special grace prevent it not.

The sadder the case of such Christians is, the more lieth upon us for their effectual recovery. We must 'restore those that are taken in a fault, in the spirit of meekness', and yet see that the sore be thoroughly searched and healed, and the joint be well set again, what pain soever it cost. We must look specially to the honour of the Gospel, and see that they rise by such full and free confessions and significations of true repentance, that some reparation be thereby made to the Church and their holy profession, for the wound of dishonour they had given it by their sin. Much skill is required to the restoring of such a soul.

4. Another part of the ministerial work is about those that are fallen under some great temptation. Much of our assistance is needful to our people in such a case. And therefore every minister should be a man that hath much insight into the Tempter's wiles. We should know the great variety of them, and the cunning craft of all Satan's instruments that lie in wait to deceive, and the methods and devices of the grand deceiver! Some of our people lie under temptations to error and heresy, especially the young, unsettled, and most self-conceited. O what a deal of holy prudence and industry is necessary in a pastor to preserve the flock from being tainted with heresies, and falling into noxious conceits and practices, and especially to keep them in unity and concord, and hinder the rising or increase of divisions.

Others lie under a temptation to worldiness, and others to gluttony or drunkenness, and others to lust; some to one sin, and some to another. A faithful pastor therefore should have his eye upon them all, and labour to be acquainted with their natural temperament, and also with their occasions and affairs in the world, and the company that they live or converse with, that so he may know where their temptations lie: and then speedily, prudently and diligently to help them.

5. Another part of our work is to comfort the discon-
solate, and to settle the peace of our people's souls, and that
on sure and lasting grounds. To which end, the quality of
the complainants, and the course of their lives had need to
be known; for all people must not have the like consolations that have the like complaints.

6. The rest of our ministerial work is upon those that
are yet strong, for they also have need of our assistance :
partly to prevent their temptations and declinings and preserve the grace they have; partly to help them for a further
progress and increase; and partly to direct them in the
improving of their strength for the service of Christ, and
the assistance of their brethren; as also to encourage them,
especially the aged, the tempted, and afflicted to hold on,
and to persevere that they may attain the crown. All these
are the objects of the ministerial work, and in respect to
all these we must 'take heed to all the flock'. *

D. We must also have a special eye upon families, to see
that they be well ordered, and the duties of each relation
performed. The life of religion and the welfare and glory
of Church and State, dependeth much on family government and duty. If we suffer the neglect of this, we undo
all. If any good be begun by the ministry in any soul in
a family, a careless, prayerless, worldly family is like to
stifle it, or very much hinder it. I beseech you therefore
to do all that you can to promote this business, as ever
you desire the true reformation and welfare of your
parishes.

Go now and then among them, when they are like to
be most at leisure, and ask the master of the family,
Whether he pray with them or read the Scripture, or what
he doth? Labour to convince the neglecters of their sin;
and if you can have opportunity, pray with them before

you go, and give them an example of what you would have them do. And get a promise of them that they will be more conscionable therein for the future.

If you find any unable to pray in tolerable expressions, through ignorance and disuse, persuade them to study their own wants and go oft to those neighbours who use to pray that they may learn, and in the mean time persuade them to use a form of prayer rather than none. Only tell them that it is to their sin and shame that they have lived so negligently as to be now so unacquainted with their own necessities, as not to know how to speak to God in prayer, when every beggar can find words to ask an alms; and therefore tell them that this form is but for necessity, as a crutch to a cripple, while they cannot do as well without it: but they must resolve not to be content with it, but to learn to do better as soon as they can, seeing prayer should come from the feeling of the heart, and be varied according to our necessities.

See that they have some profitable moving book, besides the Bible, in each family. If they have not, persuade them to buy some. If they be not able to buy them, give them some if you can; if you cannot, get some gentleman or other rich persons that are willing to do good works to do it. And engage them to read on it at nights when they have leisure, and especially on the Lord's day; direct them how to spend the Lord's day: how to despatch their worldly business, so as to prevent encumbrance and distractions, and when they have been at church, how to spend the time in their families.

Neglect not therefore this necessary part of your work: get masters of families to their duties, and they will spare you a great deal of labour with the rest, or further much the success of your labours. If a captain can get his lieutenant, cornet and other inferior officers to do their duties, he may rule the soldiers with less trouble, than if all should lie upon his hands alone. You are like to see no general reformation, till you procure family reformation. Some little obscure religion there may be in here and there one; but while it sticks in single persons, and is not promoted by these societies, it doth not prosper, nor promise much for future increase.

E. Another part of our oversight lieth in visiting the sick, and helping them to prepare for a fruitful life or a happy death. Though this should be the business of all our life and theirs, yet doth it at such a season require extraordinary care, both of them and us. When time is almost gone, and they must now or never be reconciled to God, how doth it concern them to redeem those hours, and lay hold upon eternal life! And when we see that we are like to have but a few days or hours more to speak to them, in order to their endless state, what man that is not an infidel or a block would not be much with them and do all that he can for their salvation in that short space? And as their present necessity should move us to embrace that opportunity for their good, so should the advantage that sickness and the foresight of death affordeth. There are few of the stoutest hearts but will hear us on their death bed that scorned us before. They will let fall their fury and be as tame as lambs, who were before as intractable as wasps or mad men.

If they recover, be sure to remind them of their promises. Go to them purposely to set it home; and whenever you see them remiss, go to them and mind them what they formerly said. As a bishop of Colen is said to have answered the Emperor Sigismund, when he asked him what was the way to be saved, 'He must be what he purposed, or promised, when he was last troubled with the stone and the gout.' So may we hereafter answer these.

F. Another part of this oversight is in reproving and admonishing those that live offensively or impenitently. Before we bring such matters to the congregation or a representative church, it is ordinarily most fit for the minister to try himself what he can do more privately to bow the sinner to repentance, especially if it be not a public crime. A great deal of skill is here required, and a difference must be made according to the various tempers of offenders; but with the most it will be necessary to fall on with the greatest plainness and power, to shake their careless hearts and make them see what it is to dally with sin; to let them know the evil of it, and its sad effects as regards both God and themselves.

G. [At this point Baxter inserts a long discussion of the methods of exercising 'church discipline'. Much of this is omitted here, since it is naturally related to conditions of life in the seventeenth century and has little bearing upon our present-day problems.]

The next part of our oversight consisteth in the use of church discipline: and this consisteth after the foresaid private reproofs. 1. In more public reproof. 2. And persuading the person to meet expressions of repentance. 3. And praying for them. 4. In restoring the penitent. 5. And excluding and avoiding the impenitent. My exhortation is that you would no longer neglect the execution of so much discipline in your congregations, as is confessed necessary and right. And have we been faithful in the performance of this duty? We do manifest plain laziness and sloth, if not unfaithfulness in the work of Christ. I speak from experience. It was laziness that kept me off so long, and pleaded hard against this duty. It is indeed a troublesome and painful work, and such as calls for some self-denial, because it will cast us upon the displeasure of the wicked. But dare we prefer our carnal ease, and quietness, and the love or peace of wicked men, before our service to Christ our Master?

(The neglect of discipline hath a strong tendency to the deluding of souls; by making them think they are Christians that are not, while they are permitted to live in the reputation of such, and be not separated from the rest by God's ordinance : and it may make the scandalous to think their sin a tolerable thing, which is so tolerated by the pastors of the Church.

We do corrupt Christianity itself in the eyes of the world, and do our part to make them believe that to be a Christian is but to be of such an opinion, and to have that faith which James saith the devils had; and that Christ is no more for holiness than Satan, or that the Christian religion exacteth holiness no more than the false religions of the world. For if the holy and unholy are all permitted to be sheep of the same fold, without the use of Christ's means to difference them, we do our part to defame Christ by it, as if He were guilty of it, and as if this were the strain of His prescripts.)

And for reproof these things must be observed. That the accusations of none (no not the best in the Church) be taken without proof, nor rashly entertained, nor that a minister should make himself a party, before he have sufficient evidence of the case. It is better to let many vicious persons go unpunished, or uncensured, when we want full evidence, than to censure one unjustly, which we may easily do, if we will go upon too bold presumptions.

Let there be therefore a less public meeting of chosen persons (the officers and some delegates of the Church on their behalf) to have the hearing of all such cases before they be made more public, that it may be considered whether it be just, and the offender may be dealt with then first. And if the fault be either less public, or less heinous, so that a less profession of repentance may satisfy, then if the party shall there profess repentance, it may suffice.

But if it be not so, or if the party remain impenitent, he must be reproved before all and there again invited to repentance. This duty is never the less, because our brethren have made so little conscience of the practice of it. It is not only Christ's command to tell the Church, but Paul's to rebuke such before all, and the Church hath constantly practised it till selfishness and formality caused them to be remiss in this and other duties together, and the Reformers have as much stood up for it as the rest; and as deeply are we engaged by vows, covenants, prayers and other means, for the execution of it. There is no room for a doubt, whether this be our duty, nor any to doubt whether we are unfaithful as to the performance of it. I doubt many of us that would be ashamed to omit preaching or praying, have little considered what we do in living in the wilful neglect of this duty, and the rest of discipline, so long as we have done. We little think how we have drawn the guilt of swearing, and drunkenness, and fornication, and other crimes upon our own heads, for want of using God's means for the cure of them.

If any say, There is little likelihood that public personal reprehension should do good on them, because they will be but enraged by the shame, I answer, It ill beseems the silly creature to implead the ordinances of God as useless, or to reproach His service instead of doing it, and set their wits against their Maker. God can make use of His own ordinances, or else He would never have appointed them. The usefulness of this discipline is apparent to the shaming of sin, and humbling of the sinner; and manifesting the holiness of Christ, and His doctrine and Church before all the world.

What would you have done with such sinners? Give them up as hopeless? That were too cruel. Would you use other means? Why, it is supposed that all other have been used without success, for this is the last remedy.

The principal use of this public discipline is not for the offender himself, but for the Church. It tendeth exceedingly to deter others from the like crimes, and so to keep pure the congregations and their worship.

The scorns that I have heard from many against the Scottish ministers, for bringing offenders to the stool of repentance (as if it were mere formality and hypocrisy, to take such a thing as satisfactory, when true repentance is absent) hath discovered more of the accuser's error than of theirs. For no doubt, it is true repentance that they exhort men to; and it is true repentance which offenders do profess: and whether they truly profess it, who can tell but God? It is not nothing that sin is brought to so much disgrace, and the Church doth so far acquit themselves of it.

Next, to the duty of public reproof, must be joined an exhortation of the person to repentance, and to the public profession of it for the satisfaction of the Church. For as the Church is bound to avoid communion with impenitent scandalous sinners, so when they have had the evidence of their sin, they must see some evidence of their repentance; for we cannot know them to be penitent without evidence. And what evidence is the Church capable of, but their profession of repentance first, and their actual reformation afterwards? Both which must be expected.

To these may most fitly be adjoined the public prayers

of the Church, and that both for the reproved before they are rejected, and for the rejected (some of them at least) that they may repent and be restored.

Though we have no express direction in Scripture just how long we shall stay to try whether the sinner be so impenitent as to be necessarily excluded, yet we must allow the general directions, with such diversity as the case and quality of the person shall require, it being left to the Church, who are in general to stay so long till the person manifest himself obstinate in his sin : not but that a temporal suspension may oft be inflicted in the meantime; but before we proceeded to an exclusion, it is very meet, ordinarily, that three days' prayer for him, and patience towards him should intercede.

I confess much prudence is to be exercised in such proceedings, lest we do more hurt than good; but it must be such Christian prudence as ordereth duties, and suiteth them to their ends, and not such carnal prudence as shall enervate or exclude them. It may be fit, therefore, for younger ministers to consult with others, for the more cautelous[1] proceeding in such works. And in the performance of it, we should deal humbly, even when we deal most sharply, and make it appear that it is not from any contending or lordly disposition, nor an act of revenge for any injury, but a necessary duty which we cannot conscionably avoid. And therefore it will be meet that we disclaim all such animosities, and shew the people the commands of God obliging us to what we do.

E.g., ' Neighbours and brethren, sin is so hateful an evil in the eyes of the most holy God, how light soever impenitent sinners make of it, that He hath provided the everlasting torments of Hell for the punishment of it; and no

[1] i.e. cautious.

E

lesser means can prevent the punishment than the sacrifice of the blood of the Son of God, applied to those that truly repent of it and forsake it, and therefore God that calleth all men to repentance, hath commanded us to exhort one another daily while it is called to-day, lest any be hardened through the deceitfulness of sin, and that we do not hate our brother in our heart, but in any wise rebuke our neighbour, and not suffer sin upon him : and that if our brother offend us, we should tell him his fault between him and us; and if he hear not, take two or three; and if he hear not them, tell the Church; and if he hear not the Church, he must be to us as a heathen or a publican : and those that sin, we must rebuke before all, that others may fear, and rebuke with all authority. Yea were it an apostle of Christ that should openly sin, he must be openly reproved, as Paul did Peter, and if they repent not, we must avoid them, and with such not so much as eat. According to these commands of the Lord, having heard of the scandalous practice of N.N. of this church (or parish) and having received sufficient proof that he hath committed the odious sin of ———— we have seriously dealt with him to bring him to repentance; but, to the grief of our hearts, do perceive no satisfactory success of our endeavours; but he seemeth still to remain impenitent (or still liveth in the same sin, though he verbally profess repentance). We do therefore judge it our necessary duty, to proceed in the use of that further remedy which Christ hath commanded us to try; and hence we desire him in the name of the Lord, without any further delay, to lay by his obstinacy against the Lord, and to submit to His rebuke, and will, and to lay to heart the greatness of his sin, the wrong he hath done to Christ and to himself, and the scandal and grief that he hath caused to others; and how unable he is to contend with the Almighty, and prevail against the Holy God, who to the impenitent is a consuming fire! or to save himself from His burning indignation! And I do earnestly beseech him for the sake of his own soul, that he will but soberly consider, what it is that he can gain by his sin or impenitence, and whether it will pay for the loss of everlasting life? and how he thinks to stand before God in judgment, or to appear before the Lord Jesus one of these days, when death shall snatch his soul from his body, if he be found in this impenitent state: when the Lord Jesus Himself, in whose blood they pretend to trust, hath told such with His own mouth, that except they repent they shall all perish. And I do beseech him for the sake of his own soul, and require him as a messenger of Jesus Christ, as he will answer the contrary at the bar of God, that he lay by the stoutness and impenitence of his heart, and unfeignedly confess and lament his sin before God and this congregation! And this desire I here publish, not out of any ill will to his person, as the Lord knoweth, but in love to his soul, and in obedience to Christ that hath made it my duty; desiring, that if it be possible, he may be saved from his sin, and from the power of Satan, and from the everlasting, burning wrath of God, and may be reconciled to God, and to His Church, and therefore that he may be humbled by true contrition, before he be humbled by remediless condemnation.'

Thus, or to this purpose, I conceive our public admonition should proceed: and in some cases where the sinner taketh his sin to be small, the aggravation of it will be necessary, and specially the citing of some texts of Scripture that do aggravate and threaten it.

And in case he either will not be present, that such admonition may be given to him, or will not be brought to a discovery of repentance (and to desire the prayers of

[67]

the congregation for him) it will be meet that with such a preface as this afore expressed, we desire the prayers of the congregation for him ourselves; that the people would consider what a fearful condition the impenitent are in, and have pity on a poor soul that is so blinded and hardened by sin and Satan, that he cannot pity himself; and think what it is for a man to appear before the living God in such a case, and therefore that they would join in earnest prayer to God, that He would open his eyes, and soften and humble his stubborn heart, before he be in hell beyond remedy. And accordingly let us be very earnest in prayer for them, that the congregation may be provoked affectionately to join with us; and who knows but God may hear such prayers, and the sinner's heart may more relent, than our own exhortation could procure it to do. However, the people will perceive that we make not light of sin, and preach not to them in mere custom or formality. If ministers would be conscionable in thus carrying on the work of God entirely and self-denyingly, they might make something of it, and expect a fuller blessing. But when we shrink from all that is dangerous or ungrateful, and shift off all that is costly or troublesome, they cannot expect that any great matter should be done by such a carnal, partial use of means : and though some may be here and there called home to God, yet we cannot look that the Gospel should prevail, and run, and be glorified, where it is so lamely and defectively carried on.

When a sinner is thus admonished and prayed for, if it please the Lord to open his eyes and give him remorse, before we proceed to any further censure, it is our duty to proceed to his full recovery, where these things must be observed.

·1. That we do not either discourage him by too much

severity, nor yet by too much facility and levity make nothing of discipline, nor help him to any saving cure, but merely slubber and palliate it over. If therefore he hath sinned scandalously but once, if his repentance seem deep and serious, we may in some cases restore him at that time, that is, if the wound that he hath given the credit of the Church be not so deep as to require more ado for satisfaction, or the sin so heinous as may cause us to delay. But if it be so, or if he have lived long in the sin, it is most meet that he do wait in penitence a convenient time before he be restored.

2. And when the time comes (whether at the first confession or after) it is meet that we urge him to be serious in his humiliation, and set it home upon his conscience till he seem to be truly sensible of his sin. For it is not a vain formality, but the recovery and saving of a soul that we expect.

3. We must see that he beg the communion of the Church, and their prayers to God for his pardon and salvation.

4. And that he promise to fly from such sins for the time to come.

5. And then we have these things more to do.

(*a*) To assure him of the riches of God's love, and the sufficiency of Christ's blood to pardon his sins, and that if his repentance be sincere, the Lord doth pardon him, of which we are authorized as His messengers to assure him.

(*b*) To charge him to persevere and perform his promises, and avoid temptations, and continue to beg mercy and strengthening grace.

(*c*) To charge the Church that they imitate Christ in forgiving, and retain (or if he were cast out, receive) the penitent person in their communion, and they never reproach him for his sins, or cast them in his teeth, but forgive and forget them as Christ doth.

(*d*) And then to give God thanks for his recovery so far, and to pray for his confirmation, and future preservation.

The next part of discipline is the rejecting and removing from the Church's communion those that after sufficient trial do remain impenitent. Where note,

1. That if a man have sinned but once (so scandalously) or twice, it is but a profession of repentance that we can expect for our satisfaction; but if he be accustomed to sin, or have oft broke such promises, then it is an actual reformation that we must expect. And therefore he that will refuse either of these, to reform, or to profess and manifest repentance, is to be taken by us as living in the sin. For a heinous sin, but once committed, is morally continued in till it be repented of; and a bare forbearing of the act is not sufficient.

2. Yet we have no warrant to rip up matters that are worn out of the public memory, and so to make that public again that is ceased to be public; at least in ordinary cases.

3. Exclusion from Church communion, commonly called excommunication, is of divers sorts or degrees, more than two or three, which are not to be confounded; of which I will not so far digress as here to treat.

4. That which is most commonly to be practised among us, is, Only to remove an impenitent sinner from our communion, till it shall please the Lord to give him repentance.

5. In this exclusion or removal, the minister or governors of that Church are authoritatively to charge the people in the name of the Lord to avoid communion with him; and to pronounce him one, whose communion the Church is bound to avoid: and the people's duty is obediently to avoid him, in case the pastor's charge contradict not the

word of God. So that he have the guiding or governing power; and they have (*a*) a discerning power, whether his charge be just, (*b*) and an executive power; for it's they that must execute the sentence in part, by avoiding the rejected, as he himself must execute it by denying him those ordinances and privileges not due to him, whereof he is the administrator.

6. It is very convenient to pray for the repentance and restoration, even of the excommunicate. And if God shall give them repentance, they are gladly to be received into the communion of the Church again.

Would we were but so far faithful in the practice of this discipline, as we are satisfied both of the matter and manner: and did not dispraise and reproach it by our negligence, while we write and plead for it with the highest commendations. It is worthy our consideration, Who is like to have the heavier charge about this matter at the Bar of God? Whether those deluded ones that have reproached and hindered discipline by their tongues, because they knew not its nature and necessity; or we that have so vilified it by our constant omission while with our tongues we have magnified it?

Section 2. *The Manner of this Oversight*

A. The ministerial work must be carried on prudently and orderly. Milk must go before strong meat; the foundation must be first laid before we build upon it. Children must not be dealt with as men at age. Men must be brought into a state of grace before we can expect from them the works of grace. The work of conversion and repentance from dead works, and faith in Christ, must be first and frequently and thoroughly taught. We must not ordinarily go beyond the capacities of our people, nor teach them the perfection that have not learned the principles.

B. Throughout the whole course of our ministry we must insist most upon the greatest, most certain, and most necessary truths, and be more seldom and sparing upon the rest. If we can but teach Christ to our people, we teach them all. Get them well to heaven and they will have knowledge enough. The great and commonly acknowledged truths are they that men must live upon, and which are the great instruments of raising the heart to God and destroying men's sins. It will take us off gauds and needless ornaments and unprofitable controversies to remember that one thing is necessary. Other things are desirable to be known; but this must be known or else our people are undone for ever. I confess I think necessity should be a great disposer of a minister's course of study and labour. If we were sufficient for everything, we might attempt everything, and take in order the whole Encyclopaedia : but life is short, and we are dull, and eternal things are necessary, and the souls that depend on our teaching are precious. I confess, necessity hath been the conductor of my studies and life. It chooseth what book I shall read and tells me when and how long. It chooseth my text and makes my sermon, both for matter and manner, so far as I can keep out my own corruption. Though I know the constant expectation of death hath been a great cause of this, yet I know no reason why the most healthy man should not make sure of the most necessary things first, considering the uncertainty and shortness of all men's lives.

C. All our teaching must be as plain and evident as we can make it. He that would be understood must speak to the capacity of his hearers. Truth loves the light and is most beautiful when most naked. It is a sign of an envious enemy to hide the truth; and a sign of a hypocrite to do this under pretence of revealing it; and therefore painted obscure sermons (like painted glass in windows that keeps out the light) are too oft the marks of painted hypocrites. If you would not teach men, what do you in the pulpit? If you would, why do you not speak so as to be understood? I know the height of the matter may make a man not understood, when he hath studied to make it as plain as he can; but that a man should purposely cloud the matter in strange words, and hide his mind from the people whom he pretendeth to instruct, is the way to make fools admire his profound learning and wise men his folly, pride and hypocrisy. Some men pretend necessity of it because of men's prejudices and the unpreparedness of common understandings for the truth. But truth overcomes prejudice by the mere light of evidence, and there is no better way to make a good cause prevail than to make it as plain and as generally and thoroughly known as we can. It is at best a sign that a man hath not well digested the matter himself if he is not able to deliver it plainly to another—I mean, as plainly as the nature of the matter will bear; for I know that some men cannot at present understand some truths if you speak them as plainly as words can express them; as the easiest rules in grammar, most plainly taught, will not be understood by a child that is but learning his alphabet.

D. We must so teach others as to be ready to learn of any that can teach us; not proudly venting our own conceits and disdaining all that any way contradict them, as if we had attained to the top of knowledge, and were destinated for the chair, and other men to sit at our feet. Pride is a vice that ill beseems them that must lead men in such a humble way to heaven : let us then take heed lest, when they have brought others thither, the gate should prove too strait for themselves. God that thrust out a proud angel will not entertain there a proud preacher. Methinks we should remember at least the title of a *Minister*.[1] It is this pride at the root that feedeth all the rest of our sins. Hence is the envy, the contention and unpeacableness of ministers; hence the stops in all reformation; all would lead and few will follow or concur. Hence, also, is the non-proficiency of too many ministers, because they are too proud to learn. Humility would teach them another lesson.

E. A work that requireth greater skill, and especially greater life and zeal than any of us bring to it is the public preaching of the Word. It is no small matter to stand up in the face of a congregation and to deliver a message of salvation or damnation, as from the living God, in the name of our Redeemer. It is no easy matter to speak so plain that the ignorant may understand us; and so seriously that the deadest hearts may feel us; and so convincingly that the contradicting cavillers may be silenced. The weight of our matter condemneth coldness and sleepy dulness. We should see that we be well awakened ourselves, and our spirits in such a plight as may make us fit to awaken others. If our words be not sharpened, and pierce not as nails, they will hardly be felt by stony hearts. To speak slightly and coldly of heavenly things, is near as bad as to say nothing of them.

Another part of our pastoral work is to administer the holy mysteries, or seals of God's covenant, Baptism and the Lord's Supper. A great fault it is among ourselves, that some are so careless in the manner, and others do reform that with a total neglect, and others do lay such a stress on circumstances, and make them a matter of so much

[1] i.e. the fact that it means 'servant'.

contention, even in that ordinance where union and communion is so professed.

Another part of our work is to guide our people, and be as their mouth in the public prayers of the church, and the public praises of God: as also to bless them in the name of the Lord. This sacerdotal part of the work is not the least. A great part of God's service was wont in all ages of the Church to consist in public praises and eucharistical acts in Holy Communion: and the Lord's Day was still kept as a day of thanksgiving, in the hymns and common rejoicings of the faithful, in special commemoration of the work of redemption, and the happy condition of the Gospel Church. I am as apprehensive of the necessity of preaching as some others, but yet, methinks, the solemn praises of God should take up much more of the Lord's Day than in most places they do.

F. The whole course of our ministry must be carried on in a tender love to our people. We must let them see that nothing pleaseth us but what profiteth them; and that what doeth them good doth us good; and that nothing troubleth us more than their hurt. Yea, the tenderest love of a mother should not surpass ours. We must even travail in birth, till Christ be formed in them. They should see that we care for no outward thing, not money, not liberty, not credit, not life, in comparison of their salvation; but could even be content, with Moses, to have our names blotted out of the book of life rather than that they should not be found in the Lamb's book of life. Thus should we, as John saith, be ready to 'lay down our lives for the brethren', and with Paul, not to count our lives dear unto us, so that we may but 'finish our course with joy, and the ministry which we have received of the Lord Jesus'. When the people see that you unfeignedly love them, they will hear anything and bear anything from you, and follow you the more easily.

G. All our work must be managed reverently, as beseemeth them that believe the presence of God, and use not holy things as if they were common. I know not what it doth by others, but the most reverent preacher that speaks as if he saw the face of God, doth more affect my heart, though with common words, than an irreverent man with the most exquisite preparations. Of all preaching in the world (that speaks not stark lies) I hate that preaching which tendeth to make the hearers laugh, or to move their minds with tickling levity, and affect them as stage plays use to do, instead of affecting them with a holy reverence of the name of God. We should, as it were, suppose we saw the throne of God, and the millions of glorious angels attending Him, that we may be awed with His majesty when we draw near Him in holy things, lest we profane them and take His name in vain.

(H. Moreover, if you would prosper in your work, be sure to keep up earnest desires and expectations of success. If your hearts be not set on the end of your labours, and you long not to see the conversion and edification of your hearers, and do not study and preach in hope, you are not likely to see much fruit of it.

Let all who preach for Christ and men's salvation be unsatisfied till they have the thing they preach for. He never had the right ends of a preacher that is indifferent whether he do obtain them and is not grieved when he misseth them, and rejoiced when he can see the desired issue. When a man doth only study what to say, and how, with commendation, to spend the hour, and looks for no more after it, unless it be to know what people think of his abilities, and thus holds on from year to year, I must

[76]

needs think that this man doth preach for himself and not for Christ, even when he preacheth Christ, how excellently soever he may seem to do it. I know that a faithful minister may have comfort when he wants success; and our acceptance is not according to the fruit, but according to our labour : but then, he that longeth not for the success of his labours can have none of this comfort, because he was not a faithful labourer. What I say is only for them that are set upon the end and grieved if they miss it. And this is not the full comfort that we must desire, but only such a part as may quiet us, though we miss the rest. What if God will accept a physician though the patient die? He must work in compassion and long for a better issue, and be sorry if he miss it, for all that. For it is not only our own reward that we labour for, but other men's salvation. I confess, for my part, I marvel at some ancient, reverend men that have lived twenty or forty or fifty years with an unprofitable people, among whom they have seen little fruit of their labours that it was scarce discernible, how they can, with so much patience, there go on. Were it my case, though I durst not leave the vineyard, nor quit my calling, yet I should suspect that it was God's will I should go somewhere else, and another come in my place that might be fitter for them. And I should not be easily satisfied to spend my days in such a sort.

1. Our whole work must be carried on in a sense of our insufficiency and in a pious, believing dependence on Christ. We must go to Him for light and life and strength, who sends us on the work. And when we feel our own faith weak and our hearts grown dull and unsuitable to so great a work as we have to do, we must have recourse to the Lord that sendeth us and say, 'Lord, wilt thou send me with such an unbelieving heart to persuade others to believe? Must I daily plead with sinners about everlasting life and everlasting death, and have no more belief or feeling of these weighty things myself? Oh, send me not naked and unprovided to the work; but, as Thou commandest me to do it, furnish me with a spirit suitable thereto.' Prayer must carry on our work as well as preaching : he preacheth not heartily to his people, that will not pray for them. If we prevail not with God to give them faith and repentance, we are unlikely to prevail with them to believe and repent. When our own hearts are so far out of order, and theirs so far out of order, if we prevail not with God to mend and help them, we are like to make but unsuccessful work.

J. Having given you these concomitants of our ministerial work, as singly to be performed by every minister, let me conclude with one other, that is necessary to us as we are fellow-labourers in the same work; and that is this, we must be very studious of union and communion among ourselves, and of the unity and peace of the churches that we oversee. We must be sensible how needful this is to the prosperity of the whole, the strengthening of our common cause, the good of the particular members of our flock, and the further enlargement of the Kingdom of Christ. And, therefore, ministers must smart when the Church is wounded, and be so far from being the leaders in divisions, that they should take it as a principal part of their work to prevent and heal them. Day and night should they bend their studies to find out the means to close such breaches. They must not only hearken to motions for unity, but propound them and prosecute them; not only entertain an offered peace, but even follow it when it flieth from them. They must, therefore, keep close to the ancient simplicity of the Christian faith, and the foundation and centre of

Catholic unity. They must abhor the arrogancy of them that frame new engines to rack and tear the Church of God, under pretence of obviating errors, and maintaining the truth. The Scripture sufficiency must be maintained, and nothing beyond it imposed on others; and if Papists, or others, call to us for the standard and rule of our religion, it is the Bible we must show them, rather than any confessions of Churches, or writings of men. We must learn to difference well between certainties and uncertainties, necessaries and unnecessaries, Catholic verities and private opinions; and to lay the stress of the church's peace upon the former and not upon the latter. We must avoid the common confusion of speaking of those that difference not between verbal and real errors, and that tear their brethren as heretics, before they understand them. And we must learn to see the true state of controversies, and reduce them to the very point where the difference lieth, and not make them seem greater than they are. Instead of quarrelling with our brethren, we must combine against the common adversaries; and all ministers must associate and hold communion, and correspondence, and constant meetings to these ends; and smaller differences of judgment are not to interrupt them. They must do as much of the work of God in unity and concord as they can; which is the use of synods, not to rule over one another, and make laws, but to avoid misunderstandings, and consult for mutual edification, and maintain love and communion, and go on unanimously in the work that God has already commanded us. Had the ministers of the Gospel been men of peace, and of Catholic, rather than factious spirits, the Church of Christ had not been in the case as now it is. The nations of Lutherans and Calvinists abroad, and the differing parties here at home, would not have been plotting the subversion of one another, nor remain at that distance, and in that uncharitable bitterness, nor strengthen the common enemy, and hinder the building and prosperity of the Church as they have done.

Do as much of God's work as you can in unanimity and holy concord. Blessed be the Lord that it is so well with us in this county in this regard as it is.[1] We lose our authority with our people when we divide. They will yield to us when we go together who would resist and contemn the best of us alone. Maintain your meetings for communion. Though your own person might be without the benefit of such meetings yet the Church and our common work requireth them. Do not then show yourselves contemners or neglecters of such a necessary work. Distance breedeth strangeness and fomenteth dividing flames and jealousies, which communion will prevent or cure. Ministers have need of one another and must improve the gifts of God in one another; and the self-sufficient are the most deficient, and commonly proud and empty men.

Some of them are so in love with their parties and opinions that they will not hold communion with us, because we are not of their parties; whereas by communication they might give or receive better information, or at least carry on so much of God's work in unity as we are agreed in. But the mischief of schism is to make men censorious and proud, and take others to be unmeet for their communion, and themselves to be the only Church (or pure Church) of Christ.

Section 3.   The Motives to this Oversight

Having considered the manner in which we are to take

[1] Baxter refers to the state of things in his own Worcestershire.

heed to the flock, I shall now proceed to lay before you some motives to this oversight; and here I shall confine myself to those contained in my text.

A. The first quickening consideration is taken from our relation to the flock : We are *overseers* of it.

1. The nature of our office requireth us to 'take heed to the flock'. What else are we overseers for? What a field of work is there before us! Not a person that you can see but may find you work. In the saints themselves, how do their graces languish if you neglect them? And how easily are they drawn into scandalous ways, to the dishonouring of the Gospel, and their own loss and sorrow. If this be the work of a minister, you may see what a life he hath to lead! Up, then, and let us be doing with all our might; difficulties must quicken, not discourage us in so necessary a work. If we cannot do all, let us do what we can; for, if we neglect it, woe to us, and to them.

2. Consider that you have many excellent privileges of the ministerial office to encourage you to the work. It is something that you are maintained by other men's labours. This is for your work, that you may not be taken off from it, but, as Paul requireth, may 'give yourselves wholly to these things', and not be forced to neglect men's souls, whilst you are providing for your own bodies. Either do the work, then, or take not the maintenance.

But you have far greater privileges than this. Is it nothing to be bred up to learning, when others are bred at the plough and cart, and to be furnished with so much delightful knowledge, when the world lieth in ignorance? Is it nothing to converse with learned men, and to talk of high and glorious things, when others must converse with almost none but silly ignorants? But especially, what an excellent life is it, to live in the study and preaching of

Christ!—to be still searching into His mysteries, or feeding on them!—to be daily employed in the consideration of the blessed nature, works and ways of God! Others are glad of the leisure of the Lord's day, and now and then of an hour besides, when they can lay hold of it. But we may keep a continual sabbath. We may do almost nothing else, but study and talk of God and glory and call upon Him, and drink in His sacred, saving truths. Our employment is all high and spiritual. Whether we be alone or with others, our business is for another world. Oh, were but our hearts more suitable to this work, what a blessed joyful life should we live! How sweet would our study be to us! How pleasant the pulpit! And what delight would our conference of these things afford! To live among such excellent helps as our libraries afford, to have so many silent, wise companions whenever we please—all these, and more such privileges of the ministry, bespeak our unwearied diligence in the work.

3. You are related to Christ, as well as to the flock. You are the stewards of His mysteries and rulers of His household; and He that entrusted you will maintain you in His work. But then, 'It is required of a steward that a man be found faithful.' Be true to Him, and never doubt but He will be true to you.

B. The second motive in the text is drawn from the efficient cause of this relation. It is God by His spirit that makes us overseers of His Church, and, therefore, it concerneth us to take heed to it. The Holy Ghost makes men bishops or pastors of the Church in three several respects: By qualifying them for the office; by directing the ordainers to discern their qualifications, and know the fittest men; and by directing them, the people and themselves, for the affixing them to a particular charge. It is the same Spirit still; and men are made overseers of the Church (when they are rightly called) by the Holy Ghost now as well as then. God hath determined in His word that there shall be such an office, and what the work and power of that office shall be, and what sort of men, as to their qualifications, shall receive it. None of these can be undone by man, or made unnecessary. God also giveth men the qualifications which He requireth; so that all the Church hath to do, whether pastors or people, ordainers or electors, is but to discern and determine which are the men that God hath thus qualified and to accept of them that are so provided, and, upon consent, to instal them solemnly in this office.

What an obligation, then, is laid upon us by our call to the work. If our commission is sent from heaven, it is not to be disobeyed. When the apostles were called by Christ from their secular employments, they presently left friends, and house, and trade and all, and followed Him. When Paul was called by the voice of Christ, he 'was not disobedient to the heavenly vision'. Though our call be not so immediate or extraordinary, yet it is from the same Spirit. It is no safe course to imitate Jonah in turning our back upon the commands of God. If we neglect our work He hath a spur to quicken us; if we run away from it, He hath messengers enough to overtake us and bring us back and make us do it; and it is better to do it at first than at last.

C. The third motive in the text is drawn from the dignity of the object which is committed to our charge. It is the *Church of God* which we must oversee, that Church which the world is mainly upheld for, which is sanctified by the Holy Ghost, which is the mystical body of Christ, that Church which angels are present with and attend upon as ministering spirits, whose little ones have their angels beholding the face of God in heaven. Oh what a charge is it that we have undertaken! And shall we be unfaithful to it? Have we the stewardship of God's own family, and shall we neglect it? Have we the conduct of those saints that must live for ever with God in glory, and shall we neglect them? God forbid! I beseech you, brethren, let this thought awaken the negligent. You that draw back from painful, displeasing, suffering duties, and put off men's souls with ineffectual formalities, do you think this is an honourable usage of Christ's spouse? Are the souls of men thought meet by God to see His face and live for ever in His glory, and they not worthy of your utmost cost and labour? Do you think so basely of the Church of God, as if it deserved not the best of your care and help? Christ walketh among them: remember His presence and keep all as clean as you can. They are 'a chosen generation, a royal priesthood, a holy nation, a peculiar people, to show forth the praises of Him that hath called them'. And yet dare you neglect them? What a high honour is it to be but one of them, yea, but a door-keeper in the house of God! But to be a priest of these priests, and the ruler of these kings —this is such an honour as multiplieth your obligations to diligence and fidelity in so noble an employment.

D. The last motive that is mentioned in my text, is drawn from the price that was paid for the Church which we oversee: 'Which God,' says the apostle, 'hath purchased with His own blood.' Oh what an argument is here to quicken the negligent and to condemn those who will not be quickened up to their duty by it! 'Oh,' saith one of the ancient doctors, 'if Christ had but committed to my keeping one spoonful of His blood in a fragile glass, how curiously should I preserve it, and how tender should

I be of that glass! If then He have committed to me the purchase of His blood, should I not as carefully look to my charge?' What, sirs! shall we despise the blood of Christ? Shall we think it was shed for them that are not worthy of our utmost care? You may see here, it is not a little fault that negligent pastors are guilty of. As much as in them lieth, the blood of Christ should be shed in vain. They would lose Him those souls which He hath so dearly bought.

Oh, then, let us hear these arguments of Christ, whenever we feel ourselves grow dull and careless: 'Did I die for them, and wilt thou not look after them? Were they worth My blood, and are they not worth thy labour? Did I come down from heaven to earth, to seek and to save that which was lost, and wilt thou not go to the next door, or street, or village, to seek them? How small is thy labour and condescension as to Mine? I debased Myself to this, but it is thy honour to be so employed. Have I done and suffered so much for their salvation, and was I willing to make thee a co-worker with Me, and wilt thou refuse to do that little that lieth upon thy hands?' Every time we look upon our congregations, let us believingly remember that they are the purchase of Christ's blood, and therefore should be regarded accordingly by us. And think what a confusion it will be, at the last day, to a negligent minister, to have this blood of the Son of God to be pleaded against him: and for Christ to say, 'It was the purchase of My blood that thou didst so make light of, and dost thou think to be saved by it thyself?' O brethren, seeing Christ will bring His blood to plead with us, let it plead us to our duty, lest it plead us to damnation.

I have now done with the motives which I find in the text itself. There are many more that might be gathered from the rest of this exhortation of the apostle, but we must not stay to take in all. If the Lord set home but these few upon our hearts, I dare say we shall see reason to mend our pace; and the change will be such in our hearts, and in our ministry, that ourselves and our congregations will have cause to bless God for it. I know myself unworthy to be your monitor; but a monitor you must have; and it is better for us to hear of our sin and duty from anybody than from nobody. Receive the admonition, and you will see no cause in the monitor's unworthiness to repent of it. But if you reject it, the unworthiest messenger may bear that witness against you that will confound you.

CHAPTER THREE

APPLICATION

Section 1. *The Use of Humiliation*[1]

REVEREND and dear brethren, our business here this day is to humble our souls before the Lord for our former negligence and to desire God's assistance of us in our undertaken employment for the time to come. Indeed we can hardly expect the latter without the former. If God will help us in our future duty, He will first humble us for our former sin.

We find that the guides of the Church in Scripture did confess their own sins as well as the sins of the people. Ezra confessed the sins of the priests as well as of the people, weeping and casting himself down before the house of God. Daniel confessed his own sin as well as the people's. I think if we consider well the duties already stated, and how imperfectly we have done them, we need not demur upon the question whether we have cause of humiliation. I must needs say, though I judge myself in saying it, that he that readeth but this one exhortation of Paul to the elders of the Church at Ephesus, and compareth his life with it, is too stupid and hard-hearted if he do not melt in the sense of his neglects, and be not laid in the dust before God and forced to bewail his great omissions, and to fly for refuge to the blood of Christ and to his pardoning

---

[1] The book had its origin in a Day of Humiliation—a day for humble waiting upon God in penitence and intercession.

grace. I am confident, brethren, that none of you do in judgment approve of the libertine doctrine, that crieth down the necessity of confession, contrition, and humiliation, yea, and in order to the pardon of sin. Is it not pity then that our hearts are not more orthodox as well as our heads? But I see our lesson but half learned when we know it and can say it. When the understanding hath learned it, there is more ado to teach our wills and affections, our eyes, our tongues, and hands. It is a sad thing that so many of us do use to preach our hearers asleep; but it is sadder if we have studied and preached ourselves asleep, and have talked so long against hardness of heart till our own grow hardened under the noise of our own reproofs.

And that you may see that it is not a causeless sorrow that God calleth us to I shall take it to be my duty to call to remembrance our manifold sins and set them this day in order before God and our own faces, that we may deal plainly and faithfully in a free confession of them, and that He who is faithful and just may forgive them and cleanse us from all iniquity. Wherein I suppose I have your hearty consent and that you will be so far from being offended with the disgrace of your persons and of others in this office, that you will readily subscribe the charge and be humble self-accusers; and so far am I from justifying myself by the accusation of others that I do unfeignedly put my name with the first in the bill of indictment. For how can a wretched sinner of so great transgressions presume to justify himself with God? Or how can he plead guiltless, whose conscience hath so much to say against him? If I cast shame upon the ministry, it is not on the office, but on our persons, by opening that sin which is our shame. The glory of our high employment doth not communicate any glory to our sin; for 'sin is a reproach to any people'. And be they pastors or people, it is only they that 'confess and forsake their sins that shall have mercy', while 'he that hardeneth his heart shall fall into mischief'.

[Baxter then surveys at length the sins of 'ministers of the Gospel from the days of Christ till now', in twenty-four closely printed pages, and at last arrives at his contemporaries and himself.]

The great sins that we are guilty of I shall not undertake to enumerate; and therefore my passing over any particular one is not to be taken as a denial or justification of it. But I shall take it to be my duty to give instances of some few that cry loud for humiliation and speedy reformation. Only I must needs first premise that for all the faults that are now among us I do not believe that ever England had so able and faithful a ministry since it was a nation as it hath at this day. Sure I am the change is so great within this twelve years that it is one of the greatest joys that ever I had in the world to behold it.

A. One of our most heinous and palpable sins is pride. This is a sin that hath too much interest in the best of us, but which is more hateful and inexcusable in us than in any other men. Yet is it so prevalent in some of us that it inditeth our discourses, it chooseth us our company, it formeth our countenances, it putteth the accent and emphasis upon our words. It fills some men's minds with aspiring desires and designs : it possesseth them with envious and bitter thoughts against those who stand in their light, or who by any means eclipse their glory, or hinder the progress of their reputation. Oh what a constant companion, what a tyrannous commander, what a sly and subtle insinuating enemy, is this sin of pride! It goes with men to the draper, the mercer, the tailor : it chooseth them their cloth, their trimming and their fashion. And I would that this were all or the worst. But, alas, how frequently doth it go with us to our studies, and there sit with us and do our work! How oft doth it choose our subject, and more often our words and ornaments! God biddeth us be as plain as we can, for the informing of the ignorant; and as convincing and serious as we are able for the melting and changing of unchanged hearts. And pride stands by and contradicteth all and puts in toys and trifles.

And when pride hath made the sermon, it goes with us into the pulpit, it formeth our tone, it animateth us in the delivery, it takes us off from that which may be displeasing, how necessary soever, and setteth us in a pursuit of vain applause. And the sum of all is this, it maketh men þoth in studying and preaching to seek themselves and deny God, when they should seek God's glory and deny themselves. When they should ask, What should I say and how should I say it to please God best and do most good? It makes them ask, What shall I say and how shall I deliver it to be thought a learned able preacher, and to be applauded by all that hear me? When the sermon is done, pride goeth home with them and maketh them more eager to know whether they were applauded than whether they did prevail for the saving change of souls. They could find it in their hearts but for shame, to ask folk how they liked them and to draw out their commendation. If they do perceive that they are highly thought of they rejoice, as having attained their end : but if they perceive they are esteemed but weak or common men they are displeased, as having missed the prize of the day.

But yet this is not all, nor the worst, if worse may be. Oh that ever it should be spoken of godly ministers that they are so set upon popular air, and on sitting highest in men's estimation, that they envy the parts and names of their brethren that are preferred before them, as if all were taken from their praises that is given to another; and as if God had given them His gifts to be the mere ornaments and trappings of their persons, that they may walk as men of reputation in the world, and as if all His gifts to others were to be trodden down and vilified if they seem to stand in the way of their honour. What? a saint, a preacher for Christ, and yet envy that which hath the image of Christ, and malign His gifts for which He should have the glory, and all because they seem to hinder our glory? Is not every true Christian a member of the Body, and, therefore, partaketh of the blessings of the whole, and of each particular member thereof? And doth not every man owe thanks to God for his brethren's gifts, not only as having himself a part in them, as the foot hath the benefit of the guidance of the eye; but also because his own ends may be attained by his brethren's gifts as well as by his own? For if the glory of God and the Church's felicity be not his end he is not a Christian. Will any workman malign another because he helpeth him to do his master's work? Yet, alas, how common is this heinous crime among men of parts and eminency in the Church. They can secretly blot the reputation of those that stand cross to their own; and what they cannot for shame do in plain and open terms, they will do by malicious intimations, raising suspicions where they cannot fasten accusations. And some go so far that they are unwilling that anyone that is abler than themselves should come into their pulpits, lest they should be applauded above themselves.

Hence also it comes to pass that men do so magnify their own opinions, and are as censorious of any that differ from them in lesser things: and do expect that all should be conformed to their judgments, as if they were the rules of the Church's faith! and while we cry down papal infallibility, and determination of controversies, we would too many of us be popes ourselves, and have all stand to our determination, as if we were infallible. It's true, we have more modesty than expressly to say so: we pretend that it is only the evidence of truth that appeareth in our reasons that we expect men should yield to, and our zeal is for the truth and not for ourselves. But as that must needs be taken for truth which is ours, so our reasons must needs be taken for valid; and if they be but freely examined, and found to be infirm and fallacious, and so discovered, as we are exceeding backward to see it ourselves, because they are ours, so how angry are we that it should be disclosed to others? And so we espouse the cause of our errors, as if all that were spoken against them were spoken against our persons, and we were heinously injured to have our arguments thoroughly confuted, by which we injured the truth and the minds of men! so that the matter is come to that pass through our pride, that if an error or fallacious argument do fall under the patronage of a reverend name (which is no whit rare) we must either give it the victory, and give away the truth, or else become injurious to that name that doth patronize it. For though you meddle not with their persons, yet do they put themselves under all the strokes which you give their arguments; and feel as sensibly as if you had spoken it of themselves, because they think it will follow in the eyes of men, that weak arguing is the sign of a weak man. If therefore you take it for your duty to shame their errors and false reasonings, by discovering their nakedness, they take it as if you shamed their persons; and so their names must be a garrison or fortress to their mistakes, and their reverence must defend all their sayings from the light.

And so high are our spirits, that when it becomes a duty to any man to reprove or contradict us, we are commonly impatient both of the matter and of the manner. We love the man that will say as we say, and be of our opinion, and promote our reputation, though he be less worthy of our love in other respects. But he is ungrateful to us that contradicteth us, and differeth from us, and that dealeth plainly with us in our miscarriages, and telleth us of our faults.

Brethren, I know this is a sad and harsh confession! but that all this should be so among us, should be more grievous to us than to be told of it. Could this nakedness be hid, I should not have disclosed it, at least so openly in the view of all. But alas, it is long ago open in the eyes of the world. We have dishonoured ourselves by idolizing our honour; we print our shame and preach our shame and tell it unto all. I leave every man to a cautelous jealousy and search of his own heart. But if all be graceless that are guilty of any, or many, or most of the forementioned discoveries of pride, the Lord be merciful to the ministers of this land, and give us quickly another spirit; for grace is then a rarer thing than most of us have supposed it to be.

Yet I must needs say that it is not *all* that I intend. To the praise of grace be it spoken, we have some among us that are eminent for humility and lowliness and exemplary herein to their flocks and their brethren. It is their glory and shall be their glory; and maketh them truly honourable and amiable in the eyes of God and of all good men, yea, and in the eyes of the ungodly themselves. Oh that the rest of us were but such!

Oh that the Lord would lay us at His feet in the tears

of unfeigned sorrow for this sin! Brethren, may I take leave a little to expostulate this case with my own heart and you, that we may see the shame of our sin and be reformed? Is not pride the sin of devils, the first born of hell? Is it not that wherein Satan's image doth much consist? and is it tolerable evil in men that are so engaged against him and his kingdom as we are? The very design of the Gospel doth tend to self-abasing, and the work of grace is begun and carried on in humiliation.

Humility is not a mere ornament of a Christian, but an essential part of the new creature. It is a contradiction to be a true Christian and not humble. All that will be Christians must be Christ's disciples and come to Him to learn, and their lesson is to be 'meek and lowly'. Oh how many precepts and admirable examples hath our Lord and Master given us to this end. Can one conceive of Him as purposely washing and wiping His servants' feet, and yet be stout and lordly still?

Brethren, I desire to deal closely with my own heart and yours. Have not many of us cause to enquire once and again whether sincerity will consist with such a measure of pride? When we are telling the drunkard that he cannot be saved unless he become temperate, and the fornicator that he cannot be saved unless he become chaste, have we not as great reason, if we are proud, to say of ourselves that we cannot be saved unless we become humble? Certainly, pride is a greater sin than drunkenness or whoredom; and humility is as necessary are sobriety and chastity. Truly, brethren, a man may as certainly, and more slily, make haste to hell in the way of earnest preaching of the Gospel and seeming zeal for a holy life, as in a way of drunkenness and filthiness. For what is true holiness but a devotedness to God and a living to Him? And what is a damnable state but a devotedness to our carnal selves and a living to ourselves? And doth anyone live more to himself or less to God than the proud man? And may not pride make a preacher study for himself and pray and preach and live to himself, even when he seemeth to outgo others in the work? It is not the work without the principle and end that will prove us upright. The work may be God's and yet we do it not for God but for ourselves. I confess I feel such continual danger on this point, that if I do not watch lest I should study for myself and preach for myself and write for myself, rather than for Christ, I should soon miscarry; and after all, I justify not myself when I must condemn the sin.

Consider, I beseech you, brethren, what baits there are in the work of the ministry, to entice a man to be selfish, even in the highest works of piety. The fame of a godly man is as great a snare as the fame of a learned man. But woe to him that takes up with the fame of godliness instead of godliness. 'Verily I say unto you, they have their regard.'

B. We do not so seriously, unreservedly, and laboriously lay out ourselves in the work of the Lord as beseemeth men of our profession and engagements. I bless the Lord that there are so many who do this work with all their might. But, alas! how reservedly and how negligently do the most go through their work. How few of us do so behave ourselves in our office as men that are wholly devoted thereto and have consecrated all they have to the same end. And because you shall see my grounds for this confession, I shall mention to you some of the sinful discoveries of it.

(i) It is too common with us to be negligent in our studies. Few men are at the pains that are necessary for the right informing of their understanding and fitting them for further work. Some men have no delight in their studies, but take only now and then an hour, as an unwelcome task which they are forced to undergo and are glad when they are from under the yoke. Will neither the natural desire of knowing, nor the spiritual desire of knowing God and things divine, nor the consciousness of our great ignorance and weakness, nor the sense of the weight of our ministerial work—will none of all these keep us closer to our studies, and make us more painful[1] in seeking after truth?

Oh what abundance of things are there that a minister should understand, and what a great defect it is to be ignorant of them, and how much we shall miss such knowledge in our work! Many ministers study only to compose their sermons and very little more, when there are so many books to be read and so many matters that we should not be unacquainted with. Nay, in the study of our sermons we are too negligent, gathering only a few naked truths and not considering of the most forcible expressions by which we may set them home to men's consciences and hearts. We must study how to convince and get within men, and how to bring each truth to the quick, and not leave all this to our extemporary promptitude, unless it be in cases of necessity. Certainly, brethren, experience will teach you that men are not made learned or wise without hard study and unwearied labour and experience.

(ii) If ministers were set upon the work of the Lord it would be done more vigorously than by the most of us it is. How few ministers do preach with all their might, or speak about everlasting joy or torment in such a manner

_____
[1] i.e. painstaking.

as may make men believe they are in good earnest. It would make a man's heart ache to see a company of dead, drowsy sinners sit under a minister and not have a word that is like to quicken or awaken them. The blow falls so light that hard-hearted persons cannot feel it. Most ministers will not so much as put out their voice and stir up themselves to an earnest utterance. But if they do speak loud and earnestly, how few do answer it with earnestness of matter! And then the voice doth little good; the people will take it but as mere bawling when the matter doth not correspond. It would grieve one to the heart to hear what excellent doctrine some ministers have in hand and let it die in their hands for want of close and lively application; what fit matter they have for convincing sinners, and how little they make of it and what a deal of good it might do if it were set home, and yet they cannot or will not do it.

O sirs, how plain, how close and earnestly should we deliver a message of such a nature as ours is, when the everlasting life or death of men is concerned in it. Methinks we are nowhere so wanting as in this seriousness. There is nothing more unsuitable to such a business than to be slight and dull. What! speak coldly for God and for men's salvation? Can we believe that our people must be converted or condemned and yet we speak in a drowsy tone? In the name of God, brethren, labour to awaken your hearts before you get to the pulpit, that you may be fit to waken the hearts of sinners. Though I move you not to a constant loudness in your delivery (for that will make your fervency contemptible) yet see that you have a constant seriousness; and when the matter requireth it (as it should do in the application at least) then lift up your voice and spare not your spirits.

A great matter also with the most of our hearers doth lie

[97]

G

in the very pronunciation and tone of speech. The best matter will scarce move them if it be not movingly delivered. Especially see that there be no affectation, but that we speak as familiarly to our people as we would if we were talking to any of them personally. The want of a familiar tone and expression is as great a defect in most of our deliveries as anything whatsoever, and that which we should be very careful to amend. When a man hath a reading or declaiming tone, like a schoolboy saying his lesson or an oration, few are moved with anything that he saith.

We must lay siege to the souls of sinners and find out where Satan's chief strength lieth and lay the battery of God's ordnance against it and ply it closely till a breach be made; and then suffer them not by their shifts to make it up again, but find out their common objections and give them a full and satisfactory answer. We have reasonable creatures to deal with, and as they abuse their reason against the truth so they will accept better reason for it before they will obey. We must see therefore that our sermons be all convincing, and that we make the light of Scripture and Reason shine so bright in the faces of the ungodly that it may even force them to see, unless they wilfully shut their eyes. A sermon full of mere words, how neatly soever it be composed, while there is wanting the light of evidence and the life of zeal, is but an image or a well-dressed carcase.

In preaching there is intended a communion of souls and a communication of somewhat from ours to theirs. As we and they have understandings and wills and affections, so must the bent of our endeavours be to communicate the fullest light of evidence from our understandings to theirs and to warm their hearts by kindling in them holy affections, as by a communication from our own. The great things which we have to commend to our hearers have reason enough on their side and lie plain before them in the word of God. We should, therefore, be so furnished with all store of evidence as to come as with a torrent upon their understandings and bear down all before us, and with our dilemmas and expostulations to pour shame upon all their vain objections, that they may be forced to yield to the power of truth.

C. We are sadly guilty of undervaluing the unity and peace of the whole Church. Though I scarce ever meet with anyone that will not speak for unity and peace, or, at least, that will expressly speak against it, yet it is not common to meet with those that are addicted to promote it; but too commonly do we find men averse to it, and jealous of it, if not themselves the instruments of division. It is a great and common sin throughout the Christian world to take up religion in a way of faction; and instead of a love and tender care of the universal Church, to confine that love and respect to a party.

How rare it is to meet with a man that smarteth or bleedeth with the Church's wounds, or sensibly taketh them to heart as his own, or that ever had solicitous thoughts of a cure. Almost every party thinks that the happiness of the rest consisteth in turning to them; and because they be not of their mind they cry, Down with them! and are glad to hear of their fall, as thinking that is the way to the Church's rising, that is, their own. How few there be who understand the true state of the controversies between the several parties; or that ever well discerned how many of them are but verbal, and how many are real. And if those that understand it do in order to right information and accommodation disclose it to others, it is taken as an extenuation of their errors and as a carnal compliance with them in their sin. Few men grow zealous for peace till they grow old, or have much experience of men's spirits and principles, and see better the true state of the Church and the several differences than they did before. Commonly it bringeth a man under suspicion either of favouring some heresy or abating his zeal, if he do but attempt a pacificatory work. As if there were no zeal necessary for the great fundamental verities of the Church's unity and peace, but only for parties and some particular truths.

Brethren, I speak not all this without apparent reason. We have as sad divisions among us in England, considering the piety of the persons and the smallness of the matter of our discord, as most nations under heaven have known. The most that keeps us at odds is but about the right form and order of church government. Is the distance so great that Presbyterian, Episcopal and Independent might not be well agreed? Were they but heartily willing and forward for peace, they might—I know they might. I have spoken with some moderate men of all the parties, and I perceive, by their concessions, it were an easy work. If we could not in every point agree, we might easily narrow our differences and hold communion upon our agreement in the main; determining of the safest way for the managing of our few and small disagreements, without the danger or trouble of the Church. But is this much done? It is not done. To the shame of all our faces be it spoken, it is not done. Let each party flatter themselves now as they please it will be recorded to the shame of the ministry of England, while the Gospel shall abide in the world.

And, what is the first of all, the common ignorant people take notice of all this and do not only deride us but are hardened by us against religion : and when we go about to persuade them to be religious, they see so many parties that they know not which to join; and think that it is as good to be of none at all, as of any, since they are uncertain which is the right; and thus thousands are grown into a contempt of all religion by our divisions. I know that some of these men are learned and reverend, and intend not such mischievous ends as these. The hardening of men in ignorance is not their design. But this is the thing effected. To intend well in doing ill is no rarity. Who can, in reverence to any man on earth, sit still and hold his tongue while he seeth people thus run to their own destruction and the souls of men undone by the contentions of divines for their several parties and interests?

When we once return to the ancient simplicity of faith, then, and not till then, shall we return to the ancient love and peace. I would therefore recommend to all my brethren, as the most necessary thing to the Church's peace, that they unite in necessary truths, and bear with one another in things that may be borne with; and do not make a larger creed and more necessaries than God hath done. To that end, let me entreat you to attend to the following things. 1. Lay not too great a stress upon controverted opinions, which have godly men, and, especially, whole Churches, on both sides. 2. Lay not too great a stress on those controversies that are ultimately resolvable into philosophical uncertainties, as are some unprofitable controversies about free will, the manner of the Spirit's operations and the Divine decrees. 3. Lay not too great a stress on those controversies that are merely verbal, and which if they were anatomized, would appear to be no more. Of this sort are far more (I speak it confidently upon certain knowledge) that make a great noise in the world and tear the Church, than almost any of the eager contenders that ever I spoke with do seem to discern, or are like to believe. 4. Lay not too much stress on any point of faith which was disowned by or unknown to the whole Church of Christ, in any age since the Scriptures were delivered to us. 5. Much less should you lay great stress on those of which any of the more pure and judicious ages were wholly ignorant. 6. And least of all should you lay much stress on any point which no one age since the apostles did ever receive, but all commonly held the contrary.

He that shall live to that happy time when God will heal His broken Churches, will see all this that I am pleading for reduced to practice, and this moderation take place of the new-dividing zeal, and the doctrine of the sufficiency of Scripture established; and all men's confessions and comments valued only as subservient helps, and not made the test of church communion, any further than they are the same with Scripture. Till, however, the healing age come, we cannot expect that healing truths will be entertained, because there are not healing spirits in the leaders of the church. But when the work is to be done, the workmen will be fitted for it; and blessed will be agents of so glorious a work.

I shall proceed no further in these confessions. And now, brethren, what remaineth, but that we all cry guilty of too much of these fore-mentioned sins, and humble our souls for our miscarriages before the Lord? Is this taking heed to ourselves and to all the flock? Is this like the pattern that is given us in the text? If we should now prove stout-hearted and unhumbled, how sad a symptom would it be to ourselves, and to the Church! The ministry hath oft been threatened and maligned by many sorts of adversaries; and though this may show their impious malice, yet may it also intimate to us God's just indignation. Believe it, brethren, the ministry of England are not the least nor the last in the sins of the land. It is time, therefore, for us to take our part of that humiliation to which we have been so long calling our people. If we have our wits about us, we may perceive that God hath been offended with us, and that the voice that called this nation to repentance, did speak to us as well as others. 'He that hath ears to hear, let him hear' the precepts of repentance proclaimed in so many admirable deliverances and preservations; he that hath eyes to see, let him see them written in so many lines of blood. By fire and sword hath God been calling us to humiliation; and as 'judgment hath begun at the house of God', so, if humiliation begin not there too, it will be a sad prognostication to us and to the land.

What! shall we deny or extenuate our sins, while we call our people to free and full confession? Is it not better to give glory to God by humble confession, than, in tenderness of our own glory, to seek fig leaves to cover our nakedness; and to put God to it, to build His glory, which we denied Him, upon the ruins of our own, which we preferred before Him; and to distrain for that by yet sorer judgments, which we refused voluntarily to surrender to him? Alas! if you put God to get His honour as He can, He may get it, to your greater sorrow and dishonour. Sins openly committed, are more dishonourable to us when we hide them, than when we confess them. It is the sin, and not the confession, that is our dishonour. We have committed them before the sun, so that they cannot be hid; attempts to cloak them do but increase our guilt and shame. There is no way to repair the breaches in our honour, which our sin hath made, but by free confession and humiliation. I durst not but make confession of my

own sins: and if any be offended that I have confessed
theirs, let them know, that I do but what I have done by
myself. And if they dare disown the confession of their
sin, let them do it at their peril. But as for all the truly
humble ministers of Christ, I doubt not but that they will
rather be provoked to lament their sins more solemnly, in
the face of their several congregations, and to promise
reformation.

Section 2. The Duty of Personally Catechizing and Instructing the Flock

[Baxter here has a long section on the duty of 'personal
catechizing and instructing every one in your parishes or
congregations that will submit thereto'. He had achieved
remarkable results through such systematic pastoral visitation and instruction in his own parish at Kidderminster,
and missed no opportunity of urging it upon others.[1] He
puts forward motives for the use of this method, and
answers objections, and gives some advice as to the best
way of putting it into practice. It would not be possible,
or desirable, in the very different conditions of to-day to
follow his example in detail, and no more will be given
here from this section than brief extracts. Much that he
says will be seen to be relevant to modern pastoral
visitation and the need for personal contacts.]

The last particular branch of my exhortation is, that you
will now faithfully discharge the great duty which you
have undertaken, and which is the occasion of our meeting
here to-day, in personal catechizing and instructing every
one in your parishes that will submit thereto. What our

[1] See Preface, p. 13 above, and the present editor's *Puritanism
and Richard Baxter*, p. 150 ff.

undertaking is you know, you have considered it, and it is now published to the world. But what the performance will be I know not: but I have many reasons to hope well of the most, though some will always be readier to say than to do. And because this is the chief business of the day, I must take leave to insist somewhat the longer on it. And 1. I shall give you some further motives to persuade you to faithfulness in the undertaken work; presupposing the former general motives, which should move us to this as well as to any other part of our duty. 2. I shall give to the younger of my brethren a few words of advice for the manner of the performance.

The first reasons by which I shall persuade you to this duty, are taken from the benefits of it. The second sort are taken from the difficulty. And the third from the necessity, and the many obligations that are upon us for the performance of it. And to these heads I shall reduce them all.

And for the first of these; when I look before me, and consider what, through the blessing of God, this work well managed is like to produce, it makes my heart to leap for joy. Truly, brethren, you have begun a most blessed work: and such as your own consciences may rejoice in, and your parishes rejoice in, and the nation rejoice in, and the child that is yet unborn; yea, thousands and millions for aught we know may have cause to bless God for, when we have finished our course. And though it be our business here to humble ourselves for the neglect of it so long, as we have very great cause to do, yet the hopes of a blessed success are so great in me, that they are ready to turn it into a day of rejoicing. I bless the Lord that I have lived to see such a day as this, and to be present at so solemn an engagement of so many servants of Christ to such a work. I bless the Lord that hath honoured you of this county to be the beginners and awakeners of the nation hereunto. It is not a controversial business, where the exasperated minds of divided men might pick quarrels with us, or malice itself be able to invent a rational reproach: nor is it a new invention, where envy might charge you as innovators, or proud boasters of any new discoveries of your own; or scorn to follow in it because you have led the way. No, it is a well-known duty: it is but the more diligent and effectual management of the ministerial work, and the teaching of our principles, and the feeding of babes with milk. You lead indeed, but not in invention of novelty, but the restoration of the ancient ministerial work, and the self-denying attempt of a duty that few or none can contradict.

A. Motives to this Duty.

First, it will be the most hopeful advantage for the conversion of many souls that we can expect.

The work of conversion consisteth of two parts. 1. The well informing of the judgment in the necessary points. 2. The change of the will, by the efficacy of this truth. Now in this work we have the most excellent advantage for both. For the informing of their understandings, it must needs be an excellent help to have the sum of all Christianity still in memory. We shall have the opportunity, by personal conference, to try how far they understand the catechism, and to explain it to them as we go along; and to insist on those particulars which the persons we speak to have most need to hear. So that these two conjunct—a form of words with a plain explication—may do more than either of them could do alone. They will understand a familiar speech that hear a sermon as if it were non-sense. And withal, you shall hear their objection and know where it is that Satan hath most advantage on them, and so may be able to show them their errors and confute their objections and more effectually convince them. I seldom deal with men purposely on this great business, in private serious conference, but they go away with some seeming convictions and promises of new obedience, if not some deeper remorse and sense of their condition.

If the increase of the true Church of Christ be desirable, this work is excellent, which is so likely to promote it. If you will be the fathers of many that shall be new born to God, and would see the travail of your souls with comfort, and would be able to say at last, Here am I and the children that Thou hast given me : Up then and ply this blessed work. If it will do you good, to see your holy converts among the saints in glory, and praising the Lamb before His throne; if you will be glad to present them blameless and spotless to Christ; be glad then of this singular opportunity that is offered you.

The second happy benefit of our work if well managed, will be, The most orderly building up of those that are converted, and the stablishing them in the faith.

It hazardeth the whole work, or at least much hindereth it, when we do it not in the order that it must be done. How can you build if you first lay not a good foundation? or how can you set on the top-stone if the middle parts are neglected? The second order of Christian truths have such dependence upon the first, that they can never be well learned, till the first are learned. This makes so many deluded novices, that are puffed up with vain conceits while they are grossly ignorant, and itch to be preaching before they well know what it is to be Christians; because they took not the work before them, but learnt some lesser matters which they heard most talk of, before they learnt the vital principles. And this makes many labour so much in vain, and are still learning, but never come to the knowledge of the truth, because they would learn to read before they learn to spell, or to know their letters; and this makes so many fall away, and shaken with every kind of temptation, because they were not well settled in the fundamentals. It is these fundamentals that must lead men to further truths: it is these they must bottom and build all upon. It is these that they must live upon, and that must actuate all their graces, and animate all their duties; it is these that must fortify them against particular temptations; and he that knows these well, doth know so much that will make him happy; and he that knows not these, knows nothing; and he that knows these best, is the best and most understanding Christian. The most godly people, therefore, in your congregations will find it worth their labour to learn the very words of a catechism. And if you would safely edify them, and firmly stablish them, be diligent in this work.

A third benefit that may be expected by the well-managing of the work, is this. It will make our public preaching to be better understood and regarded. When you have acquainted them with the principles, they will the better understand all that you say. They will perceive what you drive at, when they are once acquainted with the main. This prepareth their minds, and openeth you a way to their hearts: when without this you may lose the most of your labour; and the more pains you take in accurate preparations, the less good you do. As you would not therefore lose your public labour, see that you be faithful in this private work.

And this is not a contemptible benefit, that, by this course, you will come to be familiar with your people, when you have had the opportunity of familiar conference. And the want of this with us, that have very numerous parishes, is a great impediment to the success of our labours. By distance and unacquaintedness, slanderers and deceivers have opportunity to possess them with false conceits of you, which prejudice their minds against your doctrine: and by this distance and strangeness abundance of mistakes between ministers and people are fomented. Besides that, familiarity itself doth tend to beget those affections, which may open their ears to further teaching. And when we are familiar with them, they will be more encouraged to open their doubts and seek resolution, and deal freely with us. But when a minister knoweth not his people, or is as strange to them as if he did not know them, it must be a great hindrance to his doing them any good.

Besides by the means of these private instructions, we shall come to be the better acquainted with each person's spiritual state, and so the better know how to watch over them, and carry ourselves towards them ever after. We may know the better how to preach to them, when we know their temper, and their chief objections, and so what they have most need to hear. We shall the better know wherein to be jealous of them with a pious jealousy, and what temptations to help them most against. We shall the better know how to lament for them, and to rejoice with them, and to pray for them to God. For as he that will pray rightly for himself, will know his own sores and wants, and the diseases of his own heart; so he that will pray rightly for others, should know theirs as far as he may, and as is meet. If a man have the charge but of sheep or cattle, he cannot so well discharge his trust, if he know them not, and their state and qualities. So it is with the master who

[109]

will teach his scholars, and the parents who will rightly educate their children: And so with us.

Another, and one of the greatest benefits of our work, will be this, It will better inform men of the true nature of the ministerial office, or awaken them to better consideration of it, than is now usual. It is now too common for men to think that the work of the ministry is nothing but to preach well, and to baptize and administer the Lord's Supper, and visit the sick, and by this means people will submit to no more, and too many ministers are negligently or wilfully such strangers to their calling, that they will do no more. It hath oft grieved my heart to observe some eminent able preachers, how little they do for the saving of souls, save only in the pulpit; and to how little purpose much of their labour is, by this neglect. They have hundreds of people that they never spoke a word to personally for their salvation, and, if we may judge by their practice, they take it not for their duty. But I make no doubt through the mercy of God, but the restored practice of personal oversight will convince many ministers that this is as truly their work as that which they now do: and may awaken them to see that the ministry is another kind of business, than too many excellent preachers do take it to be. Brethren, do but set yourselves closely to this work, and follow on diligently, and though you do it silently, without any words to them that are negligent, I am in hope that most of you here may live to see the day, that the neglect of private personal oversight of all the flock shall be taken for a scandalous and odious omission, and shall be as disgraceful to them that are guilty of it, as preaching but once a day was heretofore. A schoolmaster must not only read a common lecture, but take a personal account of his scholars, or else he is like to do little good. If physicians should only read a public lecture of physic, their patients would not be much the better for them. Nor would a lawyer secure your estate by reading a lecture of law. The charge of pastor requireth personal dealing as well as any of these. Let us shew the world this by our practice; for most men are grown regardless of bare words.

The truth is, we have been occasioned exceedingly to wrong the Church in this, by the contrary extreme of the papists, who bring all their people to auricular confession: for in the overthrowing of this error of theirs, we have run into the contrary extreme. The people commonly think that a minister hath no more to do with them, than to preach to them, and visit them in sickness, and administer Sacraments, and that if they hear him, and receive the Sacrament from him, they owe no further obedience, nor can he require any more at their hands. Little do they know that the minister is in the church as the schoolmaster is in his school, to teach and take account of every one in particular, and that all Christians ordinarily must be disciples or scholars in some such school. They think not that a minister is in the church as a physician in a town, for all the people to resort to, for personal advice for the curing of all those diseases that are fit to be brought to a physician: and that the priest's lips must preserve knowledge, and the people must ask the law at their mouths, because he is the messenger of the Lord of Hosts. And that every soul in the congregation is bound for their own safety, to have personal recourse to him, for the resolving of their doubts; and for help against their sins, and for direction in duty, and for increase of knowledge and all saving grace! and that ministers are properly settled in congregations to this end, to be still ready to advise and help the flock. If our people did but know their duty, they

would readily come to us when they are desired to be
instructed, and to give an account of their knowledge, faith
and lives; and they would come themselves without send-
ing for, and knock oftener at our doors, and call for advice
and help for their souls; and ask, What shall we do to be
saved? Whereas now the matter is come to that sad pass,
that they think a minister hath nothing to do with them,
and if he admonish them, they will bid him look to himself,
he shall not answer for them : and if he call them to be
catechized or instructed, or to be prepared for the Lord's
Supper, or other holy ordinance, or would take account of
their faith and profiting, they will ask him, By what
authority he doth these things? and think that he is a busy
pragmatical fellow, that loves to be meddling where he
hath nothing to do; or a proud fellow that would bear rule
over their consciences. When they may as well ask him, By
what authority he preacheth, or prayeth for them, or
giveth them the Sacrament : or they may as well ask a
schoolmaster, By what authority he calls his scholars to
learn or say their lesson; Or a physician, By what authority
he enjoineth them to take his medicines? People consider
not that all our authority is but for our work : even a
power to do our duty; and our work is for them, so that
it is but an authority to do them good. And the ·silly
wretches do talk no wiselier, than if they should thus
quarrel with a man that would help to quench the fire
in their thatch, and ask him by what authority he doth
it?

What a happy thing it might be if you might live to see
the day, that it should be as ordinary for people of all ages
to come in course to their teachers for personal advice
and help for their salvation, as it is now usual for them to
come to the church, or as it is for them to send their

children thither to be catechized. Our diligence in this work is the way to do this.

B. *The Difficulties of the Work*

Difficulties we shall find many, both in ourselves and in our people, which because they are things so obvious that your experience will leave you no room to doubt of them I shall pass them over in a few words. In ourselves there is much dulness and laziness, so that there will be much ado to get us to be faithful in so hard a work. We have some of us also a foolish bashfulness which makes us backward to begin with them or to speak plainly to them. We are so modest, forsooth, that we blush to speak for Christ or to contradict the devil or to save a soul, when shameful works we are less ashamed of. We have commonly a great deal of unskilfulness and unfitness for this work. Alas! how few know how to deal with an ignorant worldly man for his conversion. To get within him and win upon him, to suit our speech to his condition and temper—who is fit for such a thing!

And many of our people will be obstinately unwilling to be taught, and scorn to come to us, as being too good to be catechized, or too old to learn, unless we deal wisely with them in public and in private, and study by the force of reason and the power of love to conquer their perverseness. And when they do come, so great is the ignorance and unapprehensiveness of many that you will find it a wonderful hard matter to get them to understand; so that if you have not the skill of making things plain you will leave them as strange to it as before. And yet harder will you find it to work things upon their hearts and to set them so home to the quick as to produce that saving change which is our end and without which our labour is almost lost.

And when all is done, the Spirit of grace must do the work.

For my own part, I apprehend that this is one of the best and greatest works I ever in my life put my hand to. I can well remember the time when I was earnest for the reformation of matters of ceremony; and if I should be cold in such a substantial matter as this, how disorderly and disproportionable would my zeal appear! Alas! can we think that the reformation is wrought when we cast out a few ceremonies and change some vestures and gestures and forms. Oh no, sirs! It is the converting and saving of souls that is our business. That is the chiefest part of reformation that doth most good and tendeth most to the salvation of the people.

I am daily forced to wonder how lamentably ignorant many of our people are who have seemed diligent hearers of me these ten or twelve years while I spoke as plainly as I was able to speak. In one hour's familiar instruction of them in private they seem to understand more than they did in all their lives before.

C. Directions for the Right Managing of this Work

The main danger arises from the want either of diligence or of skill. Of the former I have spoken much already. As for the latter I am so conscious of my own unskilfulness that I am far from imagining that I am fit to give directions to any but the younger and unexperienced of the ministry. But yet something I shall say, because the number of such is so great and I am apprehensive that the welfare of the Church and nation doth so much depend on the right management of this work.

The chief means of bringing your people to submit to this course of private catechizing or instruction is for a minister so to behave in the main course of his ministry and life as may tend to convince his people of his ability, sincerity and unfeigned love to them.

Supposing then this general preparation, the next thing to be done, is, To use the most effectual means to convince them of the benefit and necessity of this course, to their own souls. The way to win the consent of any man to any thing that you offer, is to prove it to be good for him, and to do this in evidence that hath some fitness and proportion with his own understanding. For if you cannot make him believe that it is good or necessary for him, he will never let it down, but spit it out with loathing or contempt. You must therefore preach to them some effectual convincing sermons to this purpose beforehand; which shall fully shew them the benefit and necessity of knowledge of divine truths in general, and of knowing the principles in special, and that the aged have the same duty and need as others, and in some respects much more.

When this is done, it will be very necessary that, according to our agreement, we give one of the catechisms to every family in the parish, poor and rich, so that they might be so far without excuse: For if you leave it to themselves, perhaps half of them will not so much as get them. Whereas, when they have them put into their hands, the receiving is a kind of engagement to learn them: and if they do but read the exhortation (as it's likely they will do) it will perhaps convince them, and incite them to submit. And for the delivery of them, the best way is, for the minister first to give notice in the congregation, that they shall be brought to their houses, and then to go himself from house to house and deliver them, and take the opporunity of persuading them to the work; and as they go, to take a catalogue of all the persons of years of discretion in the several families, that they may know whom they have to take care of, and instruct, and whom to expect when it cometh to their turns. I have formerly, in the distribution of some other books among them, desired every family to fetch them, but I found more confusion and uncertainty in that way, and now took this as better. But in small parishes either way may serve. Be sure that you deal gently with them; and take off all discouragements as effectually as you can.

As for the old people that are of weak memories, and not like to live long in this world, and complain that they cannot remember the words, tell them that you expect not that they should overmuch perplex their minds about it, but hear it oft read over, and see that they understand it, and get the matter into their minds and hearts, and then they may be borne with, though they remember not the words.

And let your dealings with those that you begin with, be so gentle, convincing and winning, that the report of it may be an encouragement to others to come.

Having used these means to procure them to come in and submit to your teaching, the next thing to be considered is, how you should deal most effectually with them in the work. And again I must say, that I think it is an easier matter by far, to compose and preach a good sermon, than to deal rightly with an ignorant man for his instruction in the necessary principles of religion. As much as this work is contemned by some, I doubt not but it will try the parts and spirits of ministers, and shew you the difference between one man and another, more fully than pulpit-preaching will do.

The directions which I think necessary to be observed in the managing of the work, for matter and manner, are these following.

1. When your neighbours come to you, one family or more, begin with a brief preface to demulce their minds, and take off all offence, unwillingness or discouragement, to prepare them to entertain your following instructions: e.g.

'Neighbours, it may perhaps seem to some of you as an unusual, so a troublesome business that I put you upon: but I hope you will not think it needless; for if I had thought so, I should have spared you, and myself this labour. But my conscience hath told me, yea God hath told me in His word, so roundly what it is to have the charge of men's souls, and how the blood of them that perish in their sins will be required at the hands of a minister that neglecteth them, that I dare not be so guilty of it as I have been. Alas, all our business in this world is to get well to heaven; and God hath appointed us to be guides to His people, to help them safe thither. If this be well done, all is done; and if this be not done, we are for ever undone! The Lord knows how little a while you and I may be together; and therefore it concerns us to do what we can for our own and your salvation, before we leave you or you leave the world. All other business in the world are but toys and dreams in comparison of this. The labours of your calling are but to prop up the cottages of our flesh, while you are making ready for death and judgment; which God knows is near at hand, And I hope you will be glad of help in so needful a work, and not think it much that I put you to this trouble; when the trifles of the world will not be got without further trouble.'

This, some of this, or somewhat to this purpose may tend to make them more willing to hear you, and receive instruction, or give you an account of their knowledge or practice, which must be the work of the day.

2. When you have (to spare time) spoken thus to them all, take then the persons one by one, and deal with them as far as you can in private, out of the hearing of the rest. For some cannot speak freely before others, and some will not endure to be questioned before others, because they think it tendeth to their shame to have others hear their answers; and some persons that can make better answers themselves, will be ready when they are gone to twattle of what they heard, and to disgrace those that speak not so well as they, and so people will be discouraged, and backward persons will have pretences to forbear and forsake the work, and say, they will not come to be made a scorn or a laughing stock. You must therefore be very prudent to prevent all these inconveniencies. But the main reason is, as I find by experience, people will better take plain close dealing about their sin and misery, and duty, when you have them alone, than they will before others. And if you have not opportunity to set it home and deal freely with them, you will frustrate all. If therefore you have convenient place, let the rest stay in one room, while you confer with each person by themselves in another room.

3. Let the beginning of your work be, by taking an account of what they have learned of the words of the catechism; receiving their answer to each question. And if they are able to recite but a little or none of it, try whether they can rehearse the creed and the decalogue.

This also must be observed, that if you find them at a loss and unable to answer your questions, drive them not too hard or too long with question after question, lest they conceive you intend but to puzzle them and disgrace them : but presently, when you perceive them troubled that they cannot answer, then step in yourself and take the burden off them, and make answer to the question yourselves, and then do it thoroughly and plainly, and make a full explication of the whole business to them, that by your teaching they may be brought to understand it before you leave them.

When you have either by former discovery of gross ignorance, or by latter enquiries into his spiritual state, discerned an apparent probability that the person is yet in an unconverted state, your next business is to fall on with all your skill and power to bring his heart to the sense of his condition. And here be sure if we can, to get their promise and engage them to amendment, especially to use means and change their company and forsake actual sinning, because these are more in their reach, and in this way they may wait for the accomplishing of that change that is not yet wrought. And do this solemnly, remembering them of the presence of God that heareth their promises and will expect the performance. And when you have afterward opportunity, you may remember them of that promise.

Be as serious in all, but especially in the applicatory part as you can. I scarce fear anything more than lest some careless ministers will slubber over the work and do all superficially and without life and destroy this by turning it into a mere formality: putting a few cold questions to them, and giving them two or three cold words of advice, without any life or feeling in themselves nor likely to produce any feeling in the hearers. But sure, he that valueth souls and knoweth what an opportunity is before him will do it accordingly.

[Baxter then advises at length what should be done when the minister encounters an argumentative heretic or schismatic.]

CONCLUSION

AND now, brethren, the work is before you. In these personal instructions of all the flock as well as in public preaching, doth it consist. Others have done their part, and borne their burden, and now comes in yours. What have we to do for the time to come but to deny our lazy contradicting flesh and rouse up ourselves to the business that we are engaged in. The harvest is great, the labourers are too few; the loiterers and contentious hinderers are many; the souls of men are precious: the misery of sinners is great; and the everlasting misery that they are near to is greater; the beauty and glory of the Church is desirable; the joy that we are helping them to is unconceivable; the comfort that followeth a faithful stewardship is not small; the comfort of a full success also will be greater; to be co-workers with God and His Spirit, is not a little honour; to subserve the blood-shed of Christ for men's salvation is not a light thing: to lead on the armies of Christ through the thickest of the enemies, and guide them safely through a dangerous wilderness, and steer the vessel through such storms, and rocks and sands, and shelves, and bring it safe to the harbour of rest, requireth no small skill and diligence. The fields now seem even white unto harvest, the preparations that have been made for us are very great; the season of working is more warm and calm, than most ages before us have ever seen: we have carelessly loitered too long already; the present time is posting away; while we are trifling, men are dying; how fast are men passing into another world. And is there nothing in all this to awaken us to our duty, and to resolve us to speedy and unwearied diligence?

Were there but such clear and deep impressions upon our souls, of those glorious things that we daily preach, O what a change would it make in our sermons, and in our private course! For my part, I am ashamed of my stupidity, and wonder at myself that I deal not with my own and others' souls, as one that looks for the great day of the Lord; and that I can have room for almost any other thoughts or words—and that such astonishing matters do not wholly absorb my mind. I marvel how I can preach of them slightly and coldly, and how I can let men alone in their sins, and that I do not go to them and beseech them, for the Lord's sake, to repent, however they may take it and whatever pains or trouble it may cost me. I seldom come out of the pulpit, but my conscience smiteth me that I have been no more serious and fervent in such a case. It accuseth me not so much for wants of ornament or elegancy, nor for letting fall an unhandsome word; but it asketh me, 'How couldst thou speak of life and death with such a heart? How couldst thou preach of heaven and hell in such a careless, sleepy manner? Dost thou believe what thou sayest? Art thou in earnest or in jest?' Truly this is the peal that conscience doth ring in my ears, and yet my drowsy soul will not be awakened.

O sirs, let us therefore take time while we have it and work while it is day; 'for the night cometh when no man can work.' This is our day too; and by doing good to others we must do good to ourselves. If you would prepare for a comfortable death and a sure and great reward, the harvest is before you. Gird up the loins of your minds and quit yourselves like men, that you may end your days with that confident triumph: 'I have fought a good fight, I have finished my course, I have kept the faith: henceforth there is laid up for me a crown of righteousness which the Lord, the righteous Judge, shall give unto me in that day.' If you would be blessed with those that die in the Lord, labour now that you may rest from your labours then, and do such works as you would wish should follow you, and not such as will prove your terror in the review.

What have we our time and strength for, but to lay them out for God? What is a candle made for but to burn? Burned and wasted we must be; and is it not fitter it should be in lighting men to heaven and in working for God than in living to the flesh?

THE AGREEMENT OF THE WORCESTERSHIRE ASSOCIATION

A MEETING of local ministers was held monthly in Baxter's house in Kidderminster. Some time early in 1652 he proposed that they should adopt a common plan of church discipline. With their encouragement he prepared a form of agreement, to contain 'so much of the Church Order and Discipline, as the Episcopal, Prebyterian and Independent are agreed in, as belonging to the Pastors of each particular Church'. The Agreement was accepted later by a group of central, non-party parish ministers from rather less than half of the 112 parishes in Worcestershire. The one Presbyterian minister in the county did not join, nor did any Independents, though several of them were friendly to the idea. The plan was widely taken up and similar voluntary associations were formed in at least thirteen other counties. Some such organization was particularly desirable with the breakdown of the diocesan machinery during the Commonwealth, and this movement may be regarded as an experiment towards a new church order for England, which did not have time to establish itself before the death of Cromwell. Baxter set great hopes upon these Associations as promoting the efficiency of the ministry and as a step towards that Christian unity for which he laboured all his life and with all his heart and mind. Further particulars may be found in *Richard Baxter*,

by F. J. Powicke; *The Reformed Pastor*, edited by J. T. Wilkinson, where the Agreement is reprinted in full; and in
Puritanism and Richard Baxter, by the present editor.

Baxter published the Agreement in 1653, together with
'an explication and defence', in his book, *Christian
Concord*. The first nineteen propositions in the Agreement
are concerned in great detail with the administration of
Church discipline. Proposition XX contains twenty Rules
for the conduct of the Association, the gist of which is here
reprinted:

XX. Because all Churches are parts of the Church Universal, and all true Christians are members of that body,
and of Christ; and have one Head, Lord, Faith, Baptism;
one Rule of Faith and Life, one Spirit, and one bond, and
common cognizance of entire love to Christ, and one
another; and have one Hope, one End, and must be one in
blessed union and communion with Christ everlastingly;
We judge it therefore of great and indispensable necessity,
that we use all good means for the maintaining of this
Union and Communion; and to do as much of our work
as we can in concord with one another, and as little as
may be dividedly, and by ourselves: And therefore we
resolve accordingly to our duty to keep constant communion and correspondence, and to that end to hold
certain Meetings of the Ministry in Association, and that
according to these following Rules.

1. We judge it convenient to meet in five several
Associations at five several places in this County, viz. at
Worcester, Evesham, Upton, Kidderminster and Broms-
grove, and this once a month on a day to be agreed on (or
oftener if need require).

3. We shall give notice to all Ministers of Piety, and

competent ability, who now are not an...
them to joyn with us, and offer them a fr...
thing which they may scruple, and desire t...
themselves to which Association they judge...
venient.

5. At these meetings we shall maintain some ...
tations or other Exercise, which shall be found most use...
to our own edification, especially for the younger sort
of Ministers; or else meet on purpose for this another
day.

6. We shall here endeavour on consultation to resolve
all particular doubts that arise about Discipline, or Worship, or Doctrine, which (for the avoiding of all occasions
of division) we have not thought fit to make the matter of
this Agreement or which these general Rules suffice not to
determine.

8. We shall here debate all differences in judgment (fit
for debate) that may happen among ourselves or any of
our people.

9. We shall here receive any complaint that any people
have against any member of our Association, for scandal,
false Doctrine, or maladministration; and we resolve to give
an account of our Doctrine and actions, when any offended
brother shall so accuse us, both for the satisfaction of the
Church and him.

10. We shall here make known the Names of all those
whom we have put out of our communion; and we resolve
all of us to refuse communion with such, and not to receive
them into one Church who are cast out of another, or we
first here prove them unjustly cast out.

12. We shall here make it known if there be any members of another Parish (adjoined to no Church) who desire
either Sacrament from us, that we may know from the

ster of that Place whether they are fit to be admitted or not.

14. We desire that all young Ministers, or any that are not well furnished with discretion and ability to manage those publick reproofs and censures, would do nothing in it without consulting these Assemblies, yea in so weighty a case as is excluding from Church-Communion. We judge it convenient that all Ministers advise with their Brethren of the Association for their safer proceeding.

15. We shall here consult about the good of neighbour Churches, for helping them where they want teaching, for advising them against Errors, Seducers or Scandals, and furthering to our power to propagation of the Gospel.

17. We shall once a quarter (and oftner if emergent occasion require it) send Delegates from all these Associations to Worcester (not forbidding any other to be there) where we shall hold a more general meeting for the resolving of greatest difficulties, and the more unanimous carrying on the work of the Gospel.

20. We resolve in none of our meetings to go beyond the bounds of our calling, in medling with Secular or State affairs, nor do anything injurious to the Commonwealth, but maintain all just Obedience to Authority, and shall direct all our consultations to the good of souls, the Propagation of the Gospel, the Unity, Peace and Reformation of the Church, and the glory and pleasing of God in all.

Consentimus nos infrascripti.